FRIENDS *of*
RICHMOND PARK *Guide to*
RICHMOND
PARK

First published in 2011 by The Friends of Richmond Park
www.frp.org.uk
Registered charity number 1133201

ISBN 978-0-9567469-0-0

The '1637 Enclosure Map' is taken, by permission of the author from p240 of *Palaces and Parks of Richmond and Kew Vol. I* by John Cloake. The picture of 'A tractor ploughing in the Park' appeared on p161 of Michael Baxter Brown's *Richmond Park - The History of a Royal Deer Park*, 1985, which he credited to the then Department of the Environment. 'Bomb sterilising Pit' appeared on p157 of the same book, credited to Walter Wescott.

Every effort has been made to fulfil requirements with regard to reproducing copyright material. The author will rectify any omissions at the earliest opportunity.

Edited by John Karter
jfkarter@yahoo.co.uk

Design and production by Alison Graham
The London Design Factory Ltd
design.factory@btinternet.com

Photographs on cover and pages 2, 4 and 6 by Alex Saberi http://alexsaberi.com

Printed in Malaysia for Imago

Introduction

Editing this Guide has been a labour of love. Whether I am cycling, walking, or driving through Richmond Park, it is always as if I am seeing it for the first time. Its unspoilt beauty and uniquely diverse character never fail to excite and inspire me. That this vast oasis of green - the largest enclosed urban park in Europe and as big as the seven other Royal Parks combined - should be freely accessible just a few miles from the centre of London is a perennial source of wonder to friends and visitors, especially those from overseas, who I bring to the Park as a 'must see' experience.

I was surprised to discover that there is no other current publication of a general nature about Richmond Park, so there is a clear need for the gap to be filled. The Friends' Guide sets out to do this by covering all the important aspects of the Park from flora and fauna, to history, management and 'do's and don'ts'. It is not a specialist manual, but seeks rather to offer a broad-based overview of the Park for first-time visitors and 'hardy annuals' alike. If the following pages help to increase the reader's enjoyment and understanding of this national treasure it will have achieved its objective.

John Karter, Editor. March 2011

Acknowledgements

This book would not have been possible without the help and contributions of the following people, who so generously gave their time and their work voluntarily:

Writers: Dr Nigel Reeve, Simon Richards, Jan Wilczur, Piers Eley, John Hatto, Adam Curtis, Jacqueline Shane, Jo Scrivener, Max Lankester, Michael Davison, and Ron Crompton.

Photographers: Hugh Clark, Ron Crompton, Sarah Cuttle, Kerry Davies, Sian Davies, Michael Davison, Piers Eley, Alison Graham, Steve Morgan, Susanna Ramsey, Nigel Reeve, Alex Saberi, Derek Smith, Andrew Wilson, The Royal Parks.

Special thanks go to Sir David Attenborough for writing the Foreword and for his life-long support of Richmond Park; Alison Graham of The London Design Factory, for designing and managing the production of the Guide Book with great skill and patience; Daniel Hearsum of Pembroke Lodge for allowing us access to his collection of photographs, paintings and other items pertaining to the Park; The Royal Parks for use of the map of Richmond Park and of their stock of images of the Park; Richmond Borough Council Local Studies Centre for historical illustrations; and John Cloake for reviewing the History and Buildings chapters.

Ye, who from London's smoke and turmoil fly,
To seek a purer air and brighter sky,
Think of the Bard who dwelt in yonder dell,
Who sang so sweetly what he loved so well.
Think, as ye gaze on these luxuriant bowers,
Here, Thomson loved the sunshine and the flowers.

He who could paint all their varied forms,
April's young blooms, December's dreary storms.
By yon fair stream, which calmly glides along,
Pure as his life and lovely as his song,
There oft he roved. In yonder Churchyard lies,
All of the deathless Bard that ever dies.

For here his gentle spirit lingers still,
In yon sweet vale - on this enchanted hill,
Flinging a holier interest o'er the grove,
Stirring the heart to poetry and love,
Bidding us prize the favourite scenes he trod,
And view in Nature's beauties Nature's God.

'The Seasons' by James Thomson 1700-1748

Contents

Foreword by Sir David Attenborough

I am privileged to write the foreword to this Guide. It provides just the sort of information that a new visitor wants, and the information that so many of us who use the Park regularly feel that we have at the back of our minds, but can't quite recall.

Richmond Park is a very special place for me. My regular walks in the Park (sadly very restricted nowadays), with its peace and tranquillity, have always provided me with an invaluable respite from the strains of daily life.

The Park's wildlife is exceptional, particularly for somewhere so close to a major urban centre. It well deserves its designation as a Site of Special Scientific Interest and a National Nature Reserve (given, incidentally, for its veteran trees, acid grassland and stag beetles - aspects of the Park we tend to overlook in our enthusiasm for the views and the deer).

I am particularly pleased that half of the Guide is devoted to the rich biodiversity of the Park. Richmond Park is a haven for many, especially native species of trees, grasses, invertebrates, butterflies, birds and small mammals, as well as its famous red and fallow deer.

There will always be conflict between their needs and those of human users of the Park, whose influence on the Park and present needs are covered in the second half of the Guide. It is important that the two needs are balanced, and that the special nature of the Park is preserved for future generations to enjoy, just as I have done.

David Attenborough

*The Park's savannah-type grassland
Opposite page, top inset: Deer creating
the browse-line*

Ecology of Richmond Park

By Dr Nigel Reeve, Head of Ecology, The Royal Parks.

Richmond Park is a truly remarkable ancient parkland with a wonderful blend of historic landscape and a rich wildlife. With an area of almost 2,500 acres (1,000 hectares) comprising diverse habitats such as ancient trees and decaying wood, grasslands, waterbodies and wetlands, the Park is large enough for its visitors to experience a sense of tranquillity and wilderness.

Despite its urban setting in south west London, only eight miles (13km) from London, Richmond Park's status as one of the Royal Parks has helped to ensure that its historic and natural heritage remains to be enjoyed by some two and a half million people every year. The Park's special ecological value is recognised nationally and internationally. In 1992 it was designated as London's largest Site of Special Scientific Interest (SSSI), in 2000 as a National Nature Reserve (NNR), and in 2005 as a European Special Area of Conservation (SAC).

The natural landscape, which provides us with breathtaking views through the Park and over London, owes much of its character to its geology. Areas of high ground are deposits of 'River Terrace' gravels left behind by the Thames which has repeatedly changed course and level through successive ice-ages. Over thousands of years, softer soils such as clays and silts have washed away to leave the erosion-resistant gravel terraces as high points in the landscape with stony, low nutrient soils unsuitable for agriculture.

Richmond Park's multi-layered topography, its complexity of soils and hydrology, is fundamental to the Park's scenic beauty and extraordinary diversity of habitats. Nevertheless, the management and use of the Park over the centuries – which since its enclosure in 1637 has been primarily as a deer park – have radically altered and re-shaped the natural landscape, resulting in a dynamic collage that is still changing to accommodate current and future needs.

The splendid wild herd of 630 adult Red and Fallow Deer are a delight to visitors, attracting many thousands of wildlife watchers, photographers and film crews each year. Grazing by the deer is the principal force keeping the savannah-like grasslands open and free of scrub. The deer munch away the lower branches and foliage of the trees to create a distinctive browse-line throughout the Park. Even the planting of tree species has been influenced by the needs of the deer, with standards of Sweet Chestnut and Horse Chestnut being chosen to provide an autumn fodder crop for the deer to build up their condition before the winter. Without the deer, the Park would be bereft of an essential element of its identity, landscape and ecology.

The Park consists of a mosaic of habitats, but I will focus on just three of the more significant: ancient trees and decaying wood habitats; grasslands; water-bodies and wetlands. Separate chapters in the guide deal with woodlands

and trees - which have great importance for wildlife both in the open par
and within enclosures, and, with the sensitive 'organic' management o
Park's gardens, contribute strongly to the richness of the Park's wildlife
skilfully tended gardens of Isabella Plantation and Pembroke Lodge
superb, highly accessible places to see wildlife, including woodland birds,
butterflies, bees and many other invertebrates.

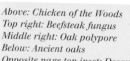

Above: Chicken of the Woods
Top right: Beefsteak fungus
Middle right: Oak polypore
Below: Ancient oaks
Opposite page top inset: Decaying wood

Ancient trees and decaying wood habitats

Richmond Park is one of the top sites for ancient trees in the UK, and indeed in Western Europe. There are ancient trees of many species in the Park, including over a thousand ancient English (Pedunculate) Oaks, some of which were already at least 200 years old when the Park was first enclosed. Many of these ancient oaks were traditionally managed by 'pollarding' in which the tree's crown was cut back at a height of about eight feet (2.5m) to stimulate the growth of foliage and new timber (regularly harvested) above the reach of browsing deer and cattle. The trees' response to regular cutting of the crown was to develop a broad trunk and a low spreading canopy. You can easily recognise these old pollards when you are in the Park.

Examine one of the ancient trees and you will see that it has rot holes and hollows, areas of exposed dead wood and peeling bark. Holes and bark flaps are essential to many of our breeding birds and roosting bats. On the trunk, you may well see the fruiting bodies of a fungus such as Chicken of the Woods or the Beefsteak fungus. Richmond Park is home to a number of rare fungi, including the Oak Polypore, a legally protected species. A specialist survey in 2008 recorded 289 different fungus species, and well over 400 species are now known from the grassland and woodland habitats in the Park. Many of these fungi form mutually beneficial associations with the roots of trees and other plants, including grasses. These 'mycorrhizal' fungi gather and supply vital nutrients from the soil in exchange for sugars and other plant products.

Fungi also play another vital role in the ecology of these ancient trees because they are some of the few kinds of organisms capable of breaking down the dead heartwood inside a tree, so freeing-up and recycling nutrients while creating a home for many different species inside the tree. The fungal fruiting bodies themselves also support an abundance of specialist species. Fungi are 'keystone' species for the ecology of the Park and protecting them is essential to the health of our trees, grassland flora and the many animals (especially invertebrates) that depend on fungi for food or habitat. This is why visitors should not take fungi from the Park but should leave mushrooms, toadstools and bracket fungi undisturbed to complete their life cycle.

About 1,400 beetle species (a third of all British beetles) have been recorded in Richmond Park; around 350 of these depend on decaying wood habitats, including scarce and threatened species such as the Cardinal Click Beetle and the Rusty Click Beetle. The wood-decaying fungi mentioned above are the key to creating the right habitat for these wonderful and rare beetles. The grubs (larvae) of Britain's largest beetle, the Stag Beetle, feed underground on decaying wood for up to six years before they pupate and emerge as adults. Undisturbed conditions are therefore vital for this internationally threatened species.

Perhaps less scenic than the ancient trees, but no less important for wildlife, are old stumps and fallen deadwood. These provide shelter for small mammals, Common Lizards, Grass Snakes, amphibians and many other creatures. Meanwhile, a whole specialised community of fungi, bacteria and invertebrates get on with the slow job of decomposing the wood and naturally recycling the nutrients. This is why we allow standing trees and fallen timber to decay naturally and undisturbed wherever possible and we ask visitors never to take wood from the Park.

Bats deserve further special mention here because of the importance of rot holes and cavities in trees as roosts for breeding and hibernation. Bats are amazing mammals that fly at night, navigating and hunting for insects using 'echolocation' calls pitched beyond the hearing range of humans. Bats have complex ecological requirements and are highly vulnerable to losses of roosting or foraging habitat, changes in insect prey availability, general disturbance and the serious disruption caused to the timing of emergence and feeding behaviour by artificial lighting. Despite a massive national decline in bat numbers since the 1950s, Richmond Park's exceptional quality of habitat is still able to support at least 9 and potentially 11 of the UK's 17 bat species.

Above top: Fallen deadwood, High Wood
Middle left: Dry grassland on thin soil
Middle right: Boggy tussock grassland
Left: Trial of cattle grazing near Holly Lodge
Opposite page top inset: Rabbits

Grasslands

Richmond Park's naturally acidic soils with low nutrient levels support a special and fragile wildlife community of fine grasses, wild flowers, fungi and invertebrates known unglamorously as 'Lowland Acid Grassland'. Characteristic fine-leaved grasses include fescues and bents, Wavy Hair Grass and Mat Grass, plus wildflowers such as Tormentil, Sheep's Sorrel and Heath Bedstraw.

Lowland Acid Grassland is a priority habitat for conservation in the UK's Biodiversity Action Plan and in London. Richmond Park contains the largest area of acid grassland in the London region. It is one of the main reasons for the Park's designation as a SSSI.

Since the Park's enclosure in the 17th century, grazing by deer has been key to maintaining the Park's extensive grasslands. Woody species, including bramble and gorse, establish quickly in any fenced enclosure that excludes grazing. A combination of grazing and variable ground conditions has fostered a valuable mosaic of grassland communities from boggy tussock grassland to dry swards on thin well-drained soils. Rabbits, voles and herbivorous invertebrates also feed on the grassland plants, but historically cattle were also significant grazing animals alongside the deer. Cattle graze in a different way to deer. Deer are very selective grazers, picking and choosing from the plants in the grassland sward. Cattle take large mouthfuls of grass, pulling up grasses and cropping the vegetation closer to the soil. This opens up the sward, reducing competition for wild flowers which can then increase in abundance and diversity. This is one reason why we are currently trialling how we might use cattle grazing to improve further the quality of our grassland habitats.

Acid grassland is not just important for its grasses and wildflowers, but also for its rich invertebrate community. In summer you may hear the buzzing courtship calls of grasshoppers and crickets; also look out for grassland butterflies, especially from June - August when most of our species are in flight. Despite the protests of some visitors, we value moderate amounts of thistle and ragwort because their flowers provide important late-summer nectar sources. Clumps of these weeds are great places to watch butterflies and other insects feeding.

In many of the Park's grassland areas you can see the mounds of ant hills, often in their hundreds. The larger mounds may be many decades old, and each is the result of many successive lifetimes of labour by thousands of tiny Yellow Meadow Ants. These fascinating ants make their living by farming subterranean aphids that suck sap from roots of plants. The mounds each contain a network of galleries within which the ants raise their young. The function of the mound is to collect warmth from the sun, and the mass of soil also acts like a storage heater to maintain a more even temperature and humidity inside.

Ant hills are of great ecological importance partly because the variation in soil conditions and micro-climate on and around the mound provides niches for

13

different species of plants and other wildlife. Several birds may feed on ants, but the most specialised is the Green Woodpecker which nests in tree holes but feeds mainly on grassland ants. A lack of disturbance is vital to conserving our anthill landscapes. Anthills cannot form in mown areas, such as the road verges, and they are very vulnerable to compaction from being stood upon, trampling and off-track cycling.

Perhaps paradoxically, some trampling and light erosion along paths is a good thing because it creates areas of bare, sun-warmed ground where many insects like to bask. On the sandier soils, these bare patches are also where the nest burrows of many of the Park's 150 or so species of solitary bees and wasps, including several national rarities, can be found.

The Invertebrate Site Register (1994) for Richmond Park lists 162 records of either 'nationally notable' or Red Data Book invertebrate species. Of over 730 species of butterflies and moths, we know of 42 species of conservation importance.

Above: Green Woodpecker feeding on anthills

This includes a robust population of the Double Line Moth, a grassland species known from only four sites in South East England. Furthermore, our continuing survey work is revealing an ever increasing list of species of conservation significance. Whatever the final statistics may be, there is no doubt that the importance of Richmond Park for invertebrate conservation is exceptionally high.

From March until July you can hear the evocative singing of Skylarks. Reed Bunting, Meadow Pipit, Stonechat and Wren are among the other ground nesting birds that also breed in the Park's grasslands. These and other birds depend for food upon the plethora of grassland invertebrates. In some areas we ask people to stay on the paths and keep dogs on a short lead during the breeding season. Thanks to those who have co-operated in this way, research by our volunteer bird recorders has shown that Skylark numbers have begun to recover. Rough tussocky grassland is also important for small mammals like Field Voles, Common and Pigmy Shrews, as well as Common Lizards and invertebrates - especially spiders which benefit from the structure of the habitat. All these species also benefit from low levels of disturbance.

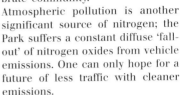

Conserving our precious acid grassland habitat depends not only on continued grazing but also on keeping soil nutrient levels low. An infertile soil is vital because it prevents the dominance of coarse grasses, stinging nettles and other plant 'thugs' that take over the habitat. Some areas of the Park have been fertilised or cultivated in the past and these are now cut for hay in late August. Harvesting the grass gradually removes the artificially added nutrients from the soil, helping a more natural grassland community gradually to develop.

A serious current threat to our acid grassland and the wildlife it supports is nutrient-enrichment (particularly nitrogen and phosphorus) from dog fouling. If you walk a dog in the Park, you can really help by always cleaning up after your dog. Because deer graze and browse within the Park, they recycle nutrients locally, whereas dogs import additional nutrients, (for example from dog food).

Top inset: Acid grassland
Below: Deer grazing in the autumn
Bracken

Deer faeces also support a specialised invertebrate community. Atmospheric pollution is another significant source of nitrogen; the Park suffers a constant diffuse 'fall-out' of nitrogen oxides from vehicle emissions. One can only hope for a future of less traffic with cleaner emissions.

Another issue in conserving our grassland habitats is the control of bracken. Bracken is no bad thing and grassland with bracken is a habitat in its own right that provides valuable breeding and refuge areas for many species. The shade of bracken benefits the native Bluebells that flourish in the Park's grasslands. Female deer choose secluded areas of bracken to hide their newborn young until they are old enough to follow their mothers. However, bracken can invade important grassland areas and shade-out the anthills. For this reason we control bracken in certain areas, mainly by cutting and rolling it. We also harvest the cut bracken to make a compost that has completely replaced the use of environmentally unfriendly peat in our horticultural work.

Water-bodies and wetlands

With about 30 ponds, many kilometres of ditches and streams, a reedbed, flooded woodland, and the two-kilometre stretch of Beverley Brook, the Park has an impressive range of wetland habitats, although little of this is truly natural. The management of water in the Park has a long history that includes the drainage of many boggy areas and the harnessing of streams using conduits and reservoirs to provide a water supply for the large houses surrounding the Park. Many of the smaller ponds were dug in the late 19th century to provide water for cattle. For example, nine ponds were added for this purpose to the Park during Josiah Parkes' major drainage and pond creation scheme between 1856 and 1861.

Small ponds and new ditches are still being created today. As the threat of climate change promises both periods of drought and torrential rain storms, the emphasis is to conserve and manage the water within the Park. This includes maintaining our water-bodies and wetlands for wildlife conservation, using and storing local water to improve sustainability (rather than using mains water) and the management of flood risk, especially flash-flooding that can occur during sudden downpours.

The Park's many ponds vary greatly in nature and their various locations, some in the open and others in deep woodland shade, provide a welcome diversity of wildlife habitats. Some ponds, such as Gallows Pond or Ham Cross Pond, may draw right down or even dry altogether in summer. Martin's Pond is one of several of these small seasonally drying ponds that are favoured by wallowing stags during the autumn rut – something well worth watching! Ponds that dry occasionally stay free of fish and are therefore ideal for frogs, toads and newts; a couple of the small ponds in the Park support Great Crested Newts, a protected species.

The largest ponds are the Upper and Lower Pen Ponds in the centre of the Park and angling is permitted here. These ponds were dug soon after the Park was enclosed, with gravel being extracted until 1683, after which they were used to rear carp for food. Resident water birds of the Pen Ponds include Coot, Moorhen, Mallard, Tufted Duck, Mute Swan, Great Crested Grebe and Grey Heron. Around any of the Park's ponds it is worth looking out for common species of damselflies like the Common Blue, Azure and Large Red damselflies and dragonflies like the Common Darter, Black-tailed Skimmer, Broad-bodied Chaser and the Southern Hawker.

The secluded south western end of the Upper Pen Pond is of particular wildlife value for its wetland habitats. There is a fine reedbed in which species such as the Reed Warbler breed each summer and one of the UK's rarest birds, the shy Bittern, has visited in several recent winters. Within the plantation behind the reedbed there are areas of flooded Willow and Alder woodland, rare habitats in the London area. Also by the Pen Ponds and in various other wet places in the Park – especially along the banks of the Beverley Brook – you can see old pollarded Crack Willows. This is another example of a tree that, under traditional management, acquires particularly high wildlife value as it ages.

The Park as it is today is not a pristine wilderness, but a collage of many changes and influences over the years. In future, its resilience, and that of its wildlife communities, will be tested by increasing human demands and by environmental changes, including climate change. Please play your part in safeguarding its future by understanding and respecting its complex ecology.

Left: Crack Willow on Beverley Brook
Below left: Rhododendron at south end of Pen Ponds
Below: Ham Gate Pond
Top inset: Martin's Pond

Deer

By Simon Richards, Park Superintendent.

Wild deer have been present in Richmond Park for thousands of years. For almost 400 years the Park has been managed as a deer park, and it is the deer that have shaped the landscape. The herd is currently maintained at 630 deer, with 300 Red and 330 Fallow deer.

In national terms, Red deer and Roe deer are the two native species. Fallow deer are certainly known to have been present in Britain in Norman times and recent studies of remains of deer found at Fishbourne Roman Palace indicate that it is probable that Fallow deer were introduced by the Romans and farmed for venison. In Victorian times the Duke of Bedford at Woburn imported several other species of deer and, of these, Sika, Muntjac and Chinese Water deer managed to escape and all have gone on to establish breeding populations in Britain. Of these, Sika deer - a close relation of Red deer - have caused a particular problem in that they can breed with Red deer and there are now many hybrids present in the wild population across Britain. It can be argued that deer parks therefore represent an important reservoir of true Red deer stock and that the Royal Parks' role is to conserve the genetic integrity of the deer as well as all the other species in the park.

With regard to terminology, male **Red deer** are stags, the females are hinds and the young are calves. Male **Fallow deer** are bucks, the female are does and the young are fawns. Whereas Red deer are always a single reddish brown colour, Fallow deer are to be found in four main colours with variants between. These are black, menil, common and white. Menil and common are the two most populous varieties; menil are distinguished by their winter coats in which the spots are retained, whereas common Fallow deer lose their spots on their winter coats.

Deer are herbivores that are well adapted to life in Richmond Park. Although grass forms the majority of their diet in summer months, they also rely heavily on foliage from the trees as well as a wider spectrum of broad-leaved plants. It is their preference for foliage that creates the particular characteristic of a deer park - the 'browse line'. This is around six feet (2m) - the height that Red deer can stand on their hind legs. They find other plants such as young gorse and brambles palatable and it is noticeable how, once mature plants are lost, the deer effectively check regeneration by eating the young shoots. Virtually no trees or shrubs grow in open parkland that have not been protected by fencing for the first few decades following planting. In the autumn the deer eat considerable quantities of acorns and beech mast (fruit of the tree), as well as conkers and sweet chestnuts. It is these four species of tree which make up the bulk of tree planting across the Park. Particular threats to any of these tree species in the future may have a marked effect on the health of the deer herds.

Picture left: Red deer hind
Top inset: Fallow deer bucks

The Park was designated as a SSSI partly in recognition of its dry acid grasslands, which are a nationally scarce habitat. This places a duty on The Royal Parks (TRP) to conserve this habitat. Although the Park has a very diverse flora, many of the species in the Park are not found in great abundance. For this reason, Natural England, who are the responsible government body charged with improving the condition of SSSIs, consider the Park to be under grazed.

This explains the recent trial of cattle grazing near Holly Lodge which commenced in 2007. Here we are seeking to establish whether cows, which graze by tearing out plants and creating open ground by trampling, as opposed to deer which browse selectively across the top of the sward, might have an important role to play in opening up bare ground in which to allow herbs to germinate and subsequently increase in abundance.

The numbers of Red and Fallow are maintained by annual deer culls. The practice is, not surprisingly, somewhat contentious, but in the absence of any realistic alternatives (contraception and relocation are commonly suggested but are neither practical nor proven), it is surely better to limit the herd by shooting than to allow the herds to proliferate and die by mass starvation. It must also be remembered that many other species depend on the presence of the deer and that removal of all deer would almost certainly have catastrophic consequences for other species which have evolved alongside them. The cull is carried out by professional Royal Parks staff and there is no stress or protracted suffering for the animals selected.

In winter months, the nutritional value of grass decreases and the deer can quite quickly lose weight and become susceptible to extreme weather conditions. Following an episode in the mid-1980s when a lot of deer died through starvation, it has been determined that the size of the deer herds should be maintained at a number around 300 Red deer and 330 Fallow deer. This ensures an adequate supply of grass. In addition, from December through to March, the deer are given an extra nightly feed consisting of a specialist deer pellet together with maize. This supplementary food ensures that the deer maintain condition through the winter.

Opposite page:
Top left: Mature Fallow bucks
Top right: Young Fallow buck
Bottom left: Young Red stag
Bottom right: Red hind

This page:
Above: Young Red stag in dust cloud
Below: Young Red stag with magpie
Top inset: Red deer on Lawn Field

One of the most distinctive features of deer is that the male animals grow antlers. An antler is a bony structure that grows annually from the pedicle (connecting structure) on top of the deer's skull. Usually towards the end of February, the largest stags begin casting their antlers; growth of new antlers commences immediately and the new tissue is quite soft and prone to damage. It has an extensive blood supply and is protected by a soft tissue known as 'velvet'. This sustains the growth of the new antler which continues until August by which time the new antler is fully grown. At this time the blood supply from the pedicle is cut off and the velvet dies off. It is at this time of the year that the deer are frequently to be seen cleaning their antlers on any available branch or fence - and when the majority of damage occurs to unprotected young trees. When the antlers are fully clean the deer are now ready for the rut.

This page:
Above: Two year old Fallow buck
Right: Young Red stag or spiker
Below: Red stags in velvet
Opposite page: bottom: Red hinds drinking at Martin's Pond
Top: Mature Red stags near White Lodge
Top inset: Mature Red stag with full antlers

In the wild, the lifespan of the deer is dictated by the wear on their teeth (in the absence of any natural predators). Deer that graze on rocky Scottish mountainsides and have a diet predominantly consisting of coarse heather wear down their teeth at a far faster rate than deer in Richmond Park and ultimately this limits their ability to graze and results in starvation.

It is commonly thought that the age of deer can be determined from the size of their antlers - and particularly by counting the points on the antlers. This is only partly true insofar as antler growth and size is influenced mainly by habitat and diet. Park deer live in a protected environment and enjoy a somewhat better diet than their truly wild relatives. It is rare for deer in the wild to live to 10 years. In the Park however the deer are in their prime between 5 and 10 years and can live beyond 10, with antler growth generally increasing each year up until this time. Beyond this, animals lose condition and subsequent antler growth regresses.

In some English deer parks, the deer have been bred selectively for many years to produce stags and bucks with massive antlers (47 points in the case of one stag at Warnham Park in Sussex). It is my opinion that these animals are grotesque and that they no longer represent the true native stag. Richmond deer generally produce no more than around 20 points at the same age as the Warnham stag. In essence the biological process is the same for bucks as it is for stags; the distinguishing feature between the two species being that whilst stags have antlers that are roughly circular in section, bucks have flattened or palmate antlers.

The rut or breeding season usually commences around the end of September and lasts for four to six weeks. The two species tend to distinguish themselves in that the dominant stags, of which there are usually around 10, maintain distinct territories around the Park and hold a group of females in their area, whereas the bucks mark their territories and invite does that are in season to come to them by virtue of their pungent scent, the immature bucks having been driven away. Once the rut has ceased, the stags tend to regroup in areas such as Spankers Hill and the females and immature animals combine into large groups that particularly favour the grasslands around Sheen Cross. Bucks generally distribute themselves in far smaller groups across the Park. Gestation is around eight months and most young are born between the end of May and mid-July. Hinds and does seek out quieter areas of the Park, which are less prone to disturbance, to give birth. The young are reckoned to be scent free for the first few days of life. This reduces their chance of predation or disturbance by dogs and humans.

Prior to the enclosure of the Park by Charles I in 1637, it is known that hunting across the area called Shene Chase was a frequent activity by the King and his entourage who were based at Hampton Court. In 1656 there were 1,500 Fallow and 200 Red deer present in the Park. Over the ensuing centuries numbers have fluctuated from over 2,000 down to 68 Fallow and 13 Red deer by the end of the Second World War. After the War, numbers recovered rapidly to over 1,000.

As can be seen from these numbers, the health of the herds has varied over time, and it has been the practice to exchange deer between some of the great deer parks of England, as well as exporting deer not only to other parks but also to foreign climes. Records show, for instance, that 133 Fallow deer were imported from Kempton Park in 1650. In recent years two bucks and two stags have been imported from Gunton Park in Norfolk with the purpose of invigorating the bloodline of the stock. Sadly both stags were casualties of the rut in 2009 when they were separately involved in fights, but their progeny can already be seen in the development of younger animals, so they have served their purpose.

Over the centuries the Park was required by Royal Warrant (along with other Royal Parks) to provide venison for the Royal table and for many other offices. These ancient rights have been fiercely protected over the centuries and can be seen to date from Norman times.

At times in the late 18th century the Royal Warrant required some 800 Fallow bucks to be killed to fulfil the entitlement. During the 20th century the Warrant was suspended during both world wars. The Royal Warrant was suspended again in 1997 and it remains to be seen whether it will ever be re-instated. At the time of suspension there was a list of some 79 offices that were still entitled to claim a haunch of venison. These varied from titles such as the Grand Falconer of England, through the Archbishop of Canterbury to the Mayor of Richmond, as well as most senior government ministers and senior civil servants. It is another long-standing tradition of this country which has fallen victim to our times. However, from a practical and economic point of view it made no sense whatsoever. Nowadays, all venison from the deer culls is advertised by public tender and sold onto the wholesale market.

It is my hope that visitors from the past centuries would still recognise Richmond Park, and that those who come after us will continue to be able to enjoy our relationship with the deer. These magnificent animals make Richmond Park a truly world class attraction.

Opposite page: top: Red stags fighting during the rut
Bottom: Red hind and young calf
This page: Top inset: Young calves
Bottom: Red stag roaring during rut

Birds
By Jan Wilczur, Richmond Park Bird Group.

Richmond Park's size and different habitats – woodlands, parkland, scrub, grassland and ponds and streams – mean it has a wide variety of birds, both resident and migrating. Altogether, 119 species of bird have been recorded in the Park, of which 57 nest here; the populations of some birds are significant in the London context.

Woodlands

The many ancient oak trees in the Park provide numerous cavities for a variety of hole-nesting birds: **Kestrel, Stock Dove, Tawny** and **Little Owls,** the 3 species of British **Woodpecker** and **Nuthatch** (which excavate their own nest-holes), **Blue Tits** and **Great Tits, Starling** and **Jackdaw**. The recently established exotic **Ring-Necked Parakeet** has increased to the point of being the most obvious bird in the Park, usurping the native Jackdaw from this position. Noisy, screeching flocks fly to and from favoured feeding areas and their communal roosts, which fortunately are located outside the Park. The effect of this large, aggressive, sociable species on native birds has yet to be assessed.

Kestrels are the most obvious bird of prey in the Park because of their habitual hovering over open areas. They tend to nest in trees at the edge of woodland. Several pairs of **Sparrowhawk** are also present, but they can be unobtrusive. In early spring, in fine weather, they perform their display flights including the roller-coasting 'sky-dance'. The subtly plumaged **Stock Dove** is mainly a summer visitor, proclaiming its territories with a double hooting call and wing-clapping display flight. Tawny Owls are resident in all the larger woodland blocks. They begin nesting early in the year when their hoots may be heard after dusk. In the late spring the hissing, begging cries of their young may be heard. In autumn hooting again becomes more frequent as established and young males vie for territory.

Green Woodpeckers and **Greater Spotted Woodpeckers** are common: the 'yaffle' of the former and the resonant drumming of the latter are characteristic sounds of the woods in early spring. The diminutive and elusive **Lesser Spotted Woodpecker** is a speciality of the Park. At least five pairs are present, but with their large territories and tendency to inhabit the treetops they are difficult to locate. The best time to do so is early spring before leaf burst. Their rapid, high-pitched 'pee-pee-pee-pee-pee' call can alert the visitor to their presence, as can their drumming which is subtly different to that of their larger relative. Two other species associated with feeding on tree trunks and larger branches, the Nuthatch and **Treecreeper**, are both fairly common.

Songbirds such as thrushes and warblers are dependent on the presence of shrubs and ground vegetation within the Park's woods. Due to the large population of deer there is little, if any, of this habitat in the unenclosed

Left: Grey heron at Pen Ponds
Top inset: Nuthatch

27

woods and they are almost devoid of songbirds. The enclosed woods hold more songbirds, such as **Blackbird, Song Thrush, Dunnock, Blackcap, Chiffchaff, Garden Warbler** and **Long-Tailed Tit**. However, large swathes of the enclosed woods are choked with non-native rhododendron, which was planted extensively many years ago for screening. It has spread throughout the woods allowing little light through to the woodland floor and preventing the growth of shrubs and ground vegetation. Even its leaves and roots contain substances toxic to other plants. The current clearance of Prince Charles' Spinney is designed to re-create some of this lost habitat.

This page:
Top: Kestrel in its nest
Right: Ring-necked Parakeet

Opposite page:
Far right: Sparrowhawk
Near right, top and bottom: Greater Spotted Woodpecker
Top inset: Green Woodpecker in flight

The best woods for songbirds are the Isabella Plantation (enclosed and with a mixture of native shrubs and formally planted areas), and Conduit Wood (unenclosed but with some small enclosed shrub areas within). Of the summering warblers, Blackcap and Chiffchaff are quite common in suitable woodland. A few pairs of Garden Warbler occur, but in private woodlands. **Willow Warblers** may stop to sing on their way north in spring but sadly, nowadays, rarely to stay to breed. A few **Spotted Flycatchers** pass through in late spring and early autumn and are another infrequent breeder. That popular harbinger of spring, the **Cuckoo**, can still just be heard in the Park. In recent years a male has proclaimed its territory in Pond Plantation. He keeps hidden in the treetops and whether he attracts a mate is usually unknown unless the bubbling call of the female is heard.

In winter, flocks of **Redwings** may be encountered. The cryptically camouflaged, crepuscular **Woodcock** also winters, but only in small numbers and is far more difficult to see. By day they hide in the large enclosed woods. At dusk they fly to their feeding areas and this is when they may be seen, but usually as silhouettes against the darkening sky. The other typical woodland birds are also present: **Wood Pigeon, Robin, Wren, Coal Tit** and **Goldcrest** where there are conifers; **Magpie, Jay and Chaffinch.**

Above: Little Owl
Right: Green Woodpecker
Below: Crow in the rubbish bins

Parkland

These are the less densely wooded parts of the Park, usually with an under-storey of bracken. The characteristic bird of this habitat is the Little Owl which occurs in a very high concentration in the Park, although they prefer areas of short grass over which to feed. They are not as strictly nocturnal as the Tawny Owl and may be seen on a sunny day perched outside their roost or nest hole. They begin feeding just before dusk when their stumpy shape may be spied on a low branch before dropping to the ground for a food item. They may continue feeding well after dawn when they have young to attend to. Sometimes young owls may be found on the ground. They are probably not orphans!

If you find a young owl on the ground, it is best not to touch it as its parents will eventually return. Most of the larger woodland birds are also found in the parkland, or wood-pasture. For reasons already explained some songbirds are less frequent, if not absent. However, the **Mistle Thrush** favours this habitat, preferring to nest high up in a tree fork and to feed in an open area. Its loud strident song can be heard in inclement weather from the end of the year onwards, earning its old country name of 'Stormcock'.

Below: Kestrel leaving its young in the nest while it hunts for food.
Top inset: Starlings in sunlight

Scrub

Apart from some isolated groups of hawthorn there is very little scrub in the Park, with the exception of two notable areas. The first of these is known as Hawthorn Valley and lies immediately north of Conduit Wood. In 2000 the few examples of hawthorn were protected from browsing by deer in small enclosures. This allowed them to develop into large bushes alongside clumps of bramble and create one of the most ornithologically interesting parts of the Park. Nearby additional enclosures were created to protect some gorse bushes. Several species of shrub-nesting birds took advantage of this new habitat, the most emblematic of these being the **Whitethroat** which performs its cheery song, sometimes in stuttering flight, when the gorse and hawthorn burst into bloom. Several other warblers occur and sometimes breed: Blackcap, Chiffchaff, Willow Warbler, the scarcer Garden Warbler, **Lesser Whitethroat** and elusive **Dartford Warbler.**

Blackbird and Song Thrush nest in the enclosures and in late autumn groups of these birds from the Continent, along with Redwings, will feast on haws and blackberries. Dunnock, Long-Tailed Tit, Chaffinch and **Goldfinch** are other residents.

Greenfinches nest in some numbers and their twittering song-flights compete with those of the Whitethroat. A variety of migrants can be found: **Stonechat, Whinchat,** Dartford Warbler, Goldcrest and the uncommon **Spotted Flycatcher.** Some of the Park's rarest visitors have been discovered here including three species of **Shrike: Great Grey, Red-Backed** and **Woodchat.** The other area of hawthorn and bramble lies alongside the road north of Kingston Gate and has been colonised by Whitethroats.

Bottom left: Reed Bunting (male)
Below: Long-tailed Tit
Bottom: Wheatear illustration

Grassland

The Park features several large open areas, some of which consist of acid grassland – a scarce and important habitat. From early spring **Skylarks** fly up high, uttering their rich and sustained song. They were on the brink of extinction as a breeding bird in the Park, mainly due to disturbance by the increasing number of visitors and their dogs, and from kite-flyers and picnickers. These ground-nesters are sensitive to disturbance because their well-hidden nests may easily be trodden upon, or the adults kept from the nest by the proximity of people, causing either the eggs to chill or even the nest to be abandoned.

Top inset: Goldfinch
Below: Common Tern

Several years ago signs were erected in the breeding seasons on Lawn Field, the remaining breeding site, asking visitors to keep to the paths and to keep dogs under control. Kite-flyers were allocated other open areas. The result has been a gradual increase in breeding pairs and the re-colonisation of other areas. The strongholds for these birds are now the grassland by the playing fields, the model-airplane flying field, and Lawn Field. It is hoped that visitors will continue to co-operate with requests to keep to paths to ensure the continued presence of this charismatic bird. Breeding birds may leave the Park for the winter, but they are replaced by birds from the Continent, at which time small flocks may be seen on the playing fields themselves.

Unfortunately, the decline of the **Meadow Pipit** has not been reversed and now only one or two pairs linger to breed on Pond Slade - Lawn Field having been vacated as a breeding site. This bird also sings in the air, but for a shorter time and has a 'parachuting' descent. However, this bird can still be numerous at other times of the year when flocks appear on migration - up to a hundred on The Bog in autumn - and in smaller numbers in winter. Large parts of grassland have been invaded by bracken, which has to be prevented from spreading into the valuable acid grassland. However, it does provide habitat for a few other species, such as Stonechat and **Reed Bunting.** The former, only ever present in small numbers in the summer, has also declined to the point of only one remaining pair. But like the Pipit, more birds occur on passage and in winter when they may be seen perching openly on bracken fronds watching out for insect food.

In recent years wintering Stonechats have been joined by Dartford Warblers which seem to enjoy their company. This heathland specialist is increasing and spreading nationally with protection and restoration of its habitat. It is, though, sensitive to harsh winters and destruction of its breeding areas by summer fires. One or both of these species may benefit from the presence of the other in having their insect prey disturbed from hiding places in the bracken. The Reed Bunting is essentially a bird of wetlands, but will also utilise drier open spaces, Pond Slade and Lawn Field being their main areas. Males sing their simple song from bracken fronds or from a nearby tree. Outside the breeding season they are far less obvious.

Whinchats only occur on passage and like to feed at the edge of bracken and grassland: The Bog, Lawn Field, Sawyer's Hill and south of White Ash Pond are the likeliest areas in which they may be found. Another bird of passage and one of the earliest to appear in spring and last to leave in autumn is the **Wheatear.** Several may be seen on The Bog - their favourite staging post. They prefer short turf over which to feed, such as that found around a rabbit warren, and may also perch on the fence of the old riding ring. Grassland also acts as an important feeding area for other birds of the Park. Green Woodpeckers can be encountered raiding anthills, along with flocks of Wood Pigeons, Jackdaws and Starlings.

The horse paddocks beside Holly Lodge serve as an important, undisturbed, feeding area for the Park's resident birds and migrant and winter visitors, where they may be viewed with ease on the short grass. Meadow Pipits will feed here when The Bog is too disturbed. Flocks of wintering Redwings and **Fieldfares** occur and **Pied Wagtails** can turn up at any time. Chaffinch, Greenfinch and Goldfinch are regularly seen around the Lodge.

Ponds and Streams

The main water bodies in the park are the Pen Ponds, Upper and Lower. Together they hold the commoner birds associated with fresh water. The largest and most obvious residents are two pairs of **Mute Swans** – one pair on each pond. They breed with varying degrees of success. The habit of the swans to take food from people causes their cygnets to be vulnerable to both dogs and foxes. If the cygnets should stray to the other pond then the male bird (cob) may attack and even kill them. In some years all the young are predated (preyed on).

A more vocal and more numerous resident is the **Canada Goose**. Up to a hundred birds of this common feral species may be present. A few pairs try to breed each year but are discouraged from doing so by the Swans. A noisier species still is the **Egyptian Goose**, a more recent addition to the country's avifauna, having escaped from collections of ornamental wildfowl. Several rather quarrelsome pairs have become established in the Park. They breed with more success than the Canada Goose, choosing to nest high up in the stumps of old trees. After hatching, the goslings jump to the ground and are escorted to the nearest pond.

Opposite page:
Bottom: Canada Geese with young

This page:
Above: Egyptian Geese with young
Left: Mute Swans on Pen Ponds
Top inset: Kingfisher illustration

One of the most attractive residents is the **Great Crested Grebe**, a pair of which usually tries to breed on one of the Ponds. In early winter they start performing their elaborate courtship ritual. The nests are built either in the reed bed at the head of Upper Pen Pond, or at the edge of an island. The stripe-headed young will ride on the backs of the parents until too large to do so, when they will then pester their parents with persistent calls to be fed. Other pairs and single birds occasionally visit. The smaller **Little Grebe** is a scarce visitor in ones and twos, usually in winter, and is unobtrusive as it tends to keep close to the reed bed.

The commonest duck in the Park is possibly the **Mandarin**, arguably one of the most beautiful birds to be found in the UK and yet another introduced species which also nests in tree holes. They prefer the ponds in the Isabella Plantation, especially Peg's Pond, but can be found elsewhere in the Park. Another common duck is the **Mallard**, again widespread in the Park. Parties of ducklings may be quickly reduced in size by a variety of predators, including **Crows, Herons,** Pike and the Red-Eared Terrapins that have made a home in Pen Ponds. Two other species of dabbling duck, which used to spend the winter in numbers of over a hundred each, are **Gadwall** and **Wigeon.** The lovely whistling call of the latter used to be a feature of the Ponds in winter. Unfortunately, probably due to the reduction in water weed, they no longer do so and are only seen now as brief visitors in small numbers. **Shoveler** and **Teal** are also occasional visitors.

Tufted Duck and **Pochard** are the two regularly seen species of diving duck with their numbers swollen in winter by birds from the Continent. Several pairs of Tufted Duck breed, their ducklings tending to appear later in the summer than the Mallard's. A few Pochard will linger through the summer and this nationally scarce breeding bird may try to nest. However, if young are hatched they are usually soon predated. The **Red-Crested Pochard** is a large, attractive ornamental duck that has escaped from collections and is establishing a feral population – a pair have tried to breed in recent years.

A characteristic and obvious bird of water bodies is the **Grey Heron:** several pairs breed in one of the enclosed plantations. Another fish-loving species is the **Cormorant**. As they now breed in London they may be seen all year either in small groups on Pen Ponds or flying over the Park.

After fishing they perch with their wings out-stretched in a heraldic pose. The raucous cries of **Black-Headed Gulls** are a feature of the Ponds in winter, although a few birds linger into spring, by which time they sport their breeding plumage of a dark brown hood. They also begin to return in mid-summer. Up to 50 of their slightly larger relative, the **Common Gull**, are true winter visitors and often give chase to their relations, forcing them to give up the bread they may have themselves poached from the wildfowl.

Opposite page:
Top left: Grey Heron feeding its young
Bottom: Great Crested Grebe in courtship display

This page:
Top inset: Mallard (male)
Below: Swans and Mallards on ice

The larger gulls, **Herring Gull, Lesser Gull** and **Greater Black-Backed Gull,** are rarely seen on the Ponds but regularly fly over the Park to and from their feeding areas and roosts on the large reservoirs in south-west London. The **Common Tern** has always been an occasional migrant and visitor from breeding colonies nearby. In 2010, a Tern raft was installed on the Upper Pond, funded by proceeds from the Visitor Centre, and a pair of Terns successfully bred on it.

At the southern end of the Upper Pond is a secluded reed bed which is home to a couple of specialities of this habitat. The **Water Rail** is a secretive relative of the more common **Coots** and **Moorhens,** more often heard than seen. Their pig-like squealing calls may be heard at dawn and dusk, especially in winter. With luck they may also be seen at these times creeping along the reed edge. Several birds winter and at least a pair probably breeds. In summer the monotonous song of several **Reed Warblers** can be heard, but again they can be difficult to see. Beyond the reed bed lies Alder Carr, another rare habitat in the Park. No special birds breed here but in autumn and winter flocks of Goldfinches, **Lesser Redpolls** and **Siskins** feed on the Alder seeds. Other birds that may pay a visit to the Ponds are the migrant **Common Sandpiper,** a wintering **Snipe, Kingfisher, Grey Wagtail** and Pied Wagtail.

From top:
Grey Heron
Red Crested Pochard (male)
Tufted Duck (male)
Shoveler (female)

Adam's Pond is the only other pond large enough to hold a range of birds. There is a resident pair of Mute Swans, Canada and Egyptian Geese, Mallard, Mandarin, **Tufted Duck,** Coot and Moorhen. Black-Headed Gulls loiter in winter. The other Ponds in the park are small and will only host either single pairs of the two geese, families of Mallard and Mandarin or a pair of Moorhens.

Beverley Brook runs through the north-east corner of the Park and is too heavily disturbed by visitors and dogs and lacks substantial vegetation around it to hold any birds. Some of the Park's water-birds will visit to feed and a pair each of Kingfishers and Grey Wagtails may breed. Up to four of the former may be seen in winter.

Top inset: Water Rail
Above: Mallard (female)
Below: Mandarin Ducks (males)

Butterflies and Day-Flying Moths

By Piers Eley, Chairman, Richmond Park Wildlife Group.

With its wild grasslands and oak and chestnut woodlands, Richmond Park is a very different environment from most of London. Its butterflies are also very different, even from those found in nearby town gardens, which are only occasional visitors to the Park. All of the Park's butterflies are beautiful and well worth looking out for when you visit.

Meadow Browns are the most common butterflies in the Park. They are members of a larger family of Browns, the Satyridae, the caterpillars of which all feed on grasses of one sort or another. Meadow Browns are to be found in the grasslands throughout the Park, where they breed in large numbers every year.

Another member of this family, the **Small Heath**, which is less than half the size of the Meadow Brown, breeds and lives in the acid grasslands. The shorter grasses and anthills that characterise this habitat, and the abundance of small yellow-flowered members of the daisy family that live there, suit it particularly well. Whereas the Meadow Brown has one brood which emerges gradually throughout the period from June to August, the Small Heath emerges in two distinct hatches, one at the end of May and a second in August.

Opposite page: Green-veined White (newly emerged by Conduit Stream).

This page:
Below left: Male Meadow Brown
Below right: Male Small Heath
Bottom left: Female Meadow Brown
Bottom right: Female Small Heath

The **Common Blue,** a cousin of the Small Copper, is another beautiful small butterfly that you may find in the same low grassy areas as the Small Copper and Small Heath. However, these butterflies also very much enjoy the flowers of thistles.

The male **Small Blue** is pictured on a flower of the creeping thistle. However, the tall marsh thistles that grow in most of the damp areas of the Park are very attractive to these and to a number of butterflies, most notably the **Painted Lady,** an occasional visitor from North Africa, whose caterpillars feed on thistle leaves. During 2009 there was an extraordinary influx of these beautiful butterflies some of which bred in the Park on the journey north.

Another small butterfly of the grasslands that emerges in two broods, one early and the other late in the summer, is the **Small Copper.** This is a spectacularly shiny orange butterfly, the colour of burnished brass. It is a much more active butterfly than the Small Heath, darting to - and - fro to challenge intruders that enter its chosen patch. It also particularly likes yellow flowers and is often to be found on ragwort. If you want to see these butterflies, your best bet is to head for each plant of ragwort that you see standing up above the grasses (deer don't eat ragwort because they don't like the smell of it, and it is poisonous to them).

This page:
Above left: Small Copper
Below left: Female Common Blue
(and inset detail)
Below right: Male Common Blue

Opposite page, from top:
Painted Lady
Gatekeeper
Small Skipper
Essex Skipper
Below far right: Male Large Skipper

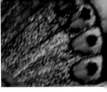

Ragwort also attracts many other types of butterfly. One of the most common of these, in its season, is the **Gatekeeper** or **Hedge Brown.** This is another member of the Brown family, and one of the most attractive, with its amber wings. Although the Gatekeeper loves ragwort, it is more closely associated with bracken and brambles in the Park, and introduces us to another set of butterflies: those to look for at the woodland edge and in clearings. All of these butterflies love the bramble flower, so look for these flowers and you may find another whole set of exciting butterflies to enjoy.

The first of these is a male **Large Skipper.** You can tell he is male by the dark sex-brands that run diagonally across his upper wings. He will emerge, each year, almost as soon as the first bramble flower opens, and will take up station nearby on a solidly placed leaf, from which he can guard his territory. He is larger than the **Small Skipper**, has more patterned wings and has a buzzing flight. The female is similar, but without the brands.

Narrow-bordered five-spot and six-spot **Burnet Moths** also enjoy thistles, as do Small Skippers and **Essex Skippers,** two other very active small butterflies that, like many of our grassland butterflies and moths, are also attracted to ragwort. The difference between the Small Skipper and its close relative, the Essex Skipper, is in the colouring of the tips of the antennae. Those of the Small Skipper are amber-coloured, while the Essex Skipper's are black. Both butterflies have quite a short season, from late June until early August, but during that time may be found in large numbers on the ragwort and thistles in their favourite locations.

The next is a recent arrival in the Park, the **Ringlet,** another of the Satyridae. This dark brown butterfly may be mistaken for the male Meadow Brown, but not if you spot the distinctive golden ringlets on the underside of its wings. You may find Ringlets on the brambles and in the grass along the damper edges of the Park, particularly alongside the Sudbrook, near Ham Gate.

The bramble flower is also attra to a number of members of Pieridae (White) family. T include the **Brimstone** and Gr **Veined White,** both of which b in the Park, unlike the much m common **Large White** and S **White,** together commonly kr as 'Cabbage Whites', with w readers will doubtless be famili

There are two more fam butterflies that you are likely to on bramble, at the woodland e the **Comma** and the **Red Adm** The Comma over-winters in Park, but the Red Admiral, lik close relation the Painted Lad mainly a long-distance mig coming over from Spain in the s and returning there in the e autumn. The **White Adm** which does not migrate, is a m rarer butterfly and a relatively arrival as a breeder in the Par also loves to feed on bramble fl ers, but, unlike the Red Adm lays its eggs on honeysuckle.

Top left: Five-spot Burnet Moth
Top right: Brimstone
Lower left: Ringlet
Below: Green-veined Whites mating

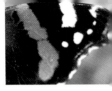

Finally, let us advance inside the woods. Here we can find two more butterflies that are very typical of Richmond Park. The first of these is the **Speckled Wood**, the last of our Satyridae, which you may spot spiralling around its rivals in leafy woodland clearings in the Park space. The second is the smaller **Purple Hairstreak**, which behaves in a similar way, spiralling round its rivals, but high up in the canopy of the oak trees, where they lay their eggs. The best time to look for these beautiful little butterflies is in the evening of a hot sunny day in July, when they are at their most active.

Left from top:
Comma
Red Admiral (and inset detail)
Peacock
Below: Speckled Wood
Bottom: Female Purple Hairstreak

The Comma and the Red Admiral both lay their eggs on nettle plants, although the Comma prefers hops, which grow wild in the Park in a few places. There are two other well-known butterflies whose caterpillars feed on nettles: the **Peacock,** which is common in the Park, and the **Small Tortoiseshell,** which has been affected by a virus and has become much less common in recent years. Both of these butterflies hibernate in the winter, as does the Comma, so they do not need to embark on the long journeys made by their two migratory cousins.

Above: Stag beetle
Below: Cardinal Click beetle
Top inset: Detail of Stag beetle

Beetles and Other Invertebrates

By John Hatto, Richmond Park Beetles Group.

The historic landscape of Richmond Park enables many beetles to survive here because of the special mix of habitats created by combining grassland, trees, open water and deer. The Park is rich in beetles that depend on decaying wood, particularly the Stag Beetle.

Beetles are the largest group - scientifically called an 'order' - of insects and form the biggest order in the entire animal kingdom, with more than 350,000 identified species worldwide. That means one in five of all named creatures is a beetle. In Britain we have more than 4,000 species and over 1,350 of these have been recorded in the site list for the Park. Beetles have been around for millions of years and are found in almost every habitat from the sea to the tops of mountains.

Beetles are insects and therefore have six legs and bodies that are divided into three sections, the head, thorax and abdomen. However, beetles are a very diverse group and vary greatly between different species in the size and in the shape of all body parts, as well as having different forms during their life cycle. Beetles also vary in size. Britain's largest terrestrial beetle is the Stag which sometimes reaches two and a half inches (6-7cm); in the Park we also have beetles that are less that a millimetre long, with many more between these extremes.

Like most insects, beetles have two pairs of wings but only use one pair for flying. The other pair has adapted to form hard covers that protect each wing when they are folded across the top of their abdomens. It should be mentioned that cockroaches are not beetles; they are related to termites and mantises.

Beetles have adapted to fill many different ecological niches. Some have also developed neat solutions to life's problems. Their bodies are encased in chitin, which forms both the soft flexible bodies of grubs and the hard structures such as legs and wing and body cases. These are strong and springy, providing good physical protection in a lightweight form. Click Beetles have a spine on the underside of the abdomen that can be snapped into a corresponding notch on the plate below the thorax. Triggering this produces a violent 'click' which can bounce the beetle into the air. Although mainly used to avoid predation, it is also useful when the beetle needs to right itself after falling on its back.

Beetles' growth and food

All species of beetles lay eggs and all undergo complete metamorphosis during their life. Female beetles' eggs are typically minute and are laid in groups which may contain a few to several thousand eggs. Parental care varies widely between species, from simply laying eggs under a leaf, to the construction of underground cells each with a supply of food (for example dung) for their young.

After hatching, the grubs go through a series of moults as they develop and grow in size in what represents the principal feeding stage of their life-cycle. At the end of the larval stage, which may last five years or more, beetles pupate, emerging fully formed from the pupa.

Different species of beetles eat different things, and the same species may eat different things at different stages of its development. The grubs of Furniture beetles eat dead wood that is dry and some people therefore think of all beetles as pests, which is not true. The grubs of the Stag beetle eat damp dead wood for the fungi it contains. However, as an adult it will only take small amounts of fluids and may live for two or three months after emerging from the ground in May or June without eating at all. Other beetles, such as Ladybirds, help control some garden pests by consuming greenfly and similar plant sap sucking insects. Many species feed on live plants, fungi and other invertebrates, but many also help break down animal and plant remains so keeping the environment healthy.

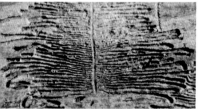

Saproxylic beetles

Saproxylic beetles are dependent on dead and decaying wood for their existence; examples are the Stag and the Cardinal Click beetles. Richmond Park has around 350 species of saproxylic beetles. Such beetles have largely disappeared from sites across Britain and mainland Europe because in the past dead wood was seen as untidy or as a danger. Yet ancient trees conserve numerous organisms that are a legacy from the days before man appeared when woodland was much more widespread. Such organisms have very specific habitat requirements and tend to be poor travellers so cannot find alternative sites to repopulate.

Dead and decaying wood is also extremely important to the health of woods and parkland. Not only is it part of nutrient recycling, providing an appropriate source of nitrogen, but in terms of climate change it is thought to play a significant role in carbon storage as well as increasing soil stability. The Richmond Biodiversity Group and The Royal Parks have produced a useful booklet on the Management of Decaying Wood.

Saproxylic beetles typically spend much of their lives deep inside trees (or in their root systems) or high above the ground. By feeding on dead wood and its fungi, they help to break down dead wood and recycle nutriments for use by existing and future trees. Richmond Park's designations as a National Nature Reserve and Site of Special Scientific Interest (SSSI) both refer to its many species of saproxylic beetles that depend on decaying wood; it is also a Special Area of Conservation for the Stag beetle.

Beetles in Richmond Park

The beetles in Richmond Park can be divided into three lifestyle groups:

1. Hunters and gatherers, such as the **Cockchafer**, **Rose Chafer**, **Great Silver Water** beetle (ponds and lakes), and the **Ladybirds**, including the invasive **Harlequin**, **Soldier**, and **Strawberry** beetles.
2. Dung dependent beetles, including the **Dor** and **Minotaur**, which can be found near rabbit warrens.
3. Saproxylic (dead and decaying wood dependent) beetles. As mentioned above, the many ancient trees in Richmond Park have helped beetles dependent on dead and decaying wood to survive. These include the **Stag** and **Lesser Stag**, the **Cardinal Click**, and the **Longhorn (Tanner)**.

Beetles and their larvae are often not very obvious in the Park. Many beetles are more active at night and because many birds eat beetles you are often more likely to find their remains than see live ones. Distinguishing between the large (about 2cm long) wing case remains of Stag beetles and Tanner beetles is mainly by upper surface colour and texture. Stags are a chestnut brown and smooth (but this beetle's size can vary by a factor of two or more.) For Tanners the wing case length to width ratio is also important as these are narrower and the colour is dark brown with ridges running top to bottom. Most predation occurs in May to July from predators such as Rooks and Jackdaws.

Opposite page:
Top left: Loggery created from dead wood
Below: Beetle galleries (marks left by larvae) on a beech tree

This page:
Below: Stag beetle pupa
Top inset: Cardinal Click beetle

There are some beetles that you are unlikely to see, but they may leave visible clues, such as the D-shaped exit hole, about 3mm in diameter, in oak trees produced by the emerging adult **Oak Jewel beetle**. These beetles are about 1cm long and lay their eggs on the bark of oak trees. The grubs bore into the living wood and feed on it, just below the bark, taking about two years to develop and pupate.

Please remember it is illegal to remove anything from the Park. Even taking wing cases removes an important means of assessing predations and in certain circumstances abundance.

A recent (2005-07) study, which was supported by many people and organisations including the Friends of Richmond Park, identified 347 species of saproxylic beetles, of which 138 have conservation status, classified as either 'notable' or one of the five 'Red Data Book' classes (categories of perceived risk). Further work continues on other invertebrates collected during that period.

From top:
Lesser Stag beetle
Rusty Click beetle
Stag beetle
Longhorn Tanner beetle (female)
Azure Damselfly
Large Red Damselfly
Below: Azure Damselfly

Opposite page:
Top inset: Detail of Azure Damselfly

Other invertebrates in the Park

There is an enormous range of invertebrates in the Park, including beetles and butterflies. Here I want to focus on dragonflies and damselflies, slugs and bees. Like butterflies, dragonflies are popular as they can be seen on warm days and there is only a limited range of species to learn. Here is a list of some species seen in the park: **Migrant Hawker, Southern Hawker, Brown Hawker, Emperor, Broad-Bodied Chaser, Black Tailed Skimmer, Common Darter, Ruddy Darter, Four Spotted Chaser.**

Dragonflies are large, powerful insects, with their wings held out at right angles whilst resting. In contrast, damselflies are typically smaller with very thin bodies, and fold their wings across their back when at rest. Those seen include: **Banded Demoiselle, Emerald, Large Red, Red Eyed, Azure, Common Blue,** and **Blue Tailed.**

You may see about nine species of **slugs** in the Park. All slugs are hermaphrodites and many have elaborate courtship rituals. That of the **Great Grey** or **Leopard slug** occurs whilst the pair are suspended on strands of mucus. Remains of similar entwined strands can be found below low trees and bushes in some protected areas in the Park. This is one of the largest keeled air-breathing land slugs in the world with an adult body length of 10-20cm. As indicated by the two common names mentioned above, their body patterning is quite variable, as is their diet, as they can be plant eaters and carnivorous on other slugs.

The Park has a wide variety of **bees and wasps,** attracted by the rich plant life. The following six species of bees can be seen regularly: **Buff-tailed Bumblebee, White-tailed Bumblebee, Garden Bumblebee, Early Bumblebee, Red-tailed Bumblebee,** and **Common Carder** bee.

As a result of the complexity of competing pressures from different users of the Park, there is a concern about possible effects on aquatic invertebrates due to the high number of dogs getting into the Park's ponds. Early draft reports on disturbance caused by dogs raise various issues. For example, some treatments for fleas in dogs contain a chemical, permethrin, which is extremely harmful to aquatic invertebrates. Another harmful effect on ponds is stirring up silt, which reduces plant and invertebrate activity, creating more silt and progressively destroying the habitat. In addition, dogs also increase bank erosion, disturb other animals and plants and can spread invasive plants from other ponds including those outside the nature reserve.

Another consequence of complexity, but one creating a measurable effect, is the serious decline in many parts of the UK in the numbers of bumblebees. Some honey bee keepers are also experiencing losses, many of which have not been explained. We do not have sufficient observers collecting data to say precisely what is happening to them in the Park.

The key message from the science of ecology is that we can no longer rely on bugs to do exactly what we want them to do. We have to work with nature not against it and we need more sites like Richmond Park where the needs of wildlife and a healthy ecosystem are given priority.

Brown Long-Eared bat
and also opposite page, top inset

Bats

By Adam Curtis, Assistant Park Manager.

Richmond Park supports at least 9 of the UK's 17 bat species, each adapted to different habitat niches. The Park provides a vital continuity of environment and relatively low disturbance.

The **Brown Long-Eared** bat has short, wide wings with a large flight surface and hovers in woodland canopies, gleaning moths from the underside of leaves. **Noctule, Leisler's** and **Serotine** bats have long, thin wings enabling efficient fast flight in straight lines - ideal for catching large flying insects (including Chafers and Stag beetles) high above the wood or in open parkland.

Daubenton's bat has large feet and a broad tail membrane used to catch insects from the surface of water-bodies. Its fur is waxy and water-proof; needed when its hunting fails and it ends up in the water! The three species of **Pipistrelle** (**Common, Nathusius'** and **Soprano**) bats depend on midges, eating as many as 3,000 per night.

In order to fly, bats need to keep their weight down, which restricts them from carrying heavy fat reserves. They need regular feeds and conserve fuel by lowering their metabolism during the day and by hibernating when the temperature is below four degrees celsius. They navigate and locate their insect prey at night by echolocation (the location of objects by reflected sound) at frequencies above human hearing. Each 'squeak' is timed with wing-beats and exhalation to further maximize fuel use. They may live up to 30 years, have just one pup annually, and depend on tree cavities and buildings for hibernation, mating and maternity roosts.

To think of bats as 'flying mice' shows a lack of appreciation of their complex ecological and social needs. Unlike rodents, bats' survival rests on a knife edge - they are vulnerable to bright lights, disturbance, habitat loss and landscape changes - and their populations have plummeted since the 1950s. This is why all UK bats and their roost sites are now protected under law.

Richmond Park has changed relatively little over time and has provided that vital continuity of habitat and tree cavities for over 400 years. Only the very rare **Barbastelle** bat has been pushed to extinction here, because its requirements could only be met by a landscape much larger than the Park. Nonetheless the Park remains an exceptional site for bats including uncommon species such as Leisler's, Nathusius' Pipistrelle and **Natterer's** bats. The Park is also large enough to fully support a large breeding population of Brown Long-Eared bats. They are particularly vulnerable to urban light pollution because they hunt in shadows using conventional sight and cannot fly long distances to dark areas. They survive well on 'Richmond Park Island' surrounded by an urban sea of London light.

Common Pipistrelle

Trees

By Adam Curtis, Assistant Park Manager.

Richmond Park has about 130,000 trees in its woodlands and parkland. The veteran **Oaks**, *the tall boundary* **Beeches** *and the younger plantations of mixed species create unique atmospheres, supporting a vast array of wildlife. They define the landscape's character, filtering out the presence of London. They shelter our long country walks, creating intrigue and intimacy, enticing us deep into contemplation. When a man is tired of London there is nothing more restorative than a woodland walk in Richmond Park.*

Perhaps surprisingly, this 'natural' landscape has been created over 1,000 years of active management. Most of the Park's trees have been deliberately planted by past managers and their motives were often rooted in commercial interest. Our woodland heritage is a mixture of features superimposed on each other, creating a rich and varied treescape distributed over different areas, including:

- Open parkland - mostly grassland with very occasional trees
- Well treed parkland - a scattering of well spaced trees in grassland areas
- Unenclosed woodlands - densely planted woodlands where trees have competed for light and grown tall and straight
- Enclosed woodlands - as above but fenced from deer, so should have more ground flora and trees below six feet (2m)
- Riparian woodlands - tree species specialised to grow on wet ground
- Scrub enclosures - small areas of low, dense Hawthorn or Gorse cover
- Rhododendron cover - distributed under some of the woodlands

The economics of woodland management have changed over the past 1,000 years and, in the time it took for trees to mature, witnessed a change in society and how we value trees. In the past, the trees were often valued for their monetary benefits - in shipbuilding, firewood or food for deer for hunting. Nowadays we value the Park as a nature reserve and public open space and the trees are valued and managed for their non-monetary benefits.

Main picture: Veteran Oak
Right: Crack Willows at Pen Ponds
Top inset: Beech tree new growth

Natural regeneration

Understanding the Park's tree cover is helped by an appreciation of deer park ecology. Deer browse rather than graze - by preference they find woody vegetation more palatable than grass. They quickly consume new seedlings and the low hanging foliage on trees. Deer parks have an absence of shrubs and are held in a state of equilibrium with their characteristic 'browse-line' on the trees - a neatly trimmed line to the base of the tree crown.

Natural regeneration of trees is very limited and only those protected from deer will mature. We can be confident that only the trees older than the 1637 enclosure could have seeded naturally. All other trees have been planted or at least protected from deer until mature. The Park's three-sided deer guards and uniform browse-line are the tell-tale signs in photographs frequently seen in newspapers and television weather reports. All woodland blocks were originally protected, even if the fence has long since fallen down.

Historically the Park's main purpose was the production of venison. Trees that bore large seeds would provide vital feed to bring the deer safely through the winter. A large proportion of the Park's trees provide such food, but thereafter the composition is rather eclectic. Not only are there good native timber trees; we can also find exotic species and ornamental plantings.

Composition of tree species in the Park

Of Richmond Park's trees, 45% are Oaks, another 20% are Beech, and 5% are **Sweet** and **Horse Chestnut**. Their acorns, beech mast (fruit), conkers and chestnuts provide a critical part of the deer diet. **Hawthorn, Birch** and **Hornbeam** together are another 20%, meaning that 90% of the trees in the Park come from just seven species. The remaining 10% are a variety of indigenous and exotic species, from **Willows** and **Alders** to 18th century **Cedars** and 20th century **Sugar Maples.**

The Park has a low percentage of trees that bear small seeds, berries or blossom. Associated wildlife that depend on these food groups are relatively less abundant. However, Birch does naturally regenerate inside enclosures where it finds protection from deer and supports a number of small birds whose bills are adapted for small seeds such as Siskins, Lesser Redpolls and Goldfinches. There are also plenty of Hawthorn trees that contribute blossoms in spring and berries in autumn.

This page: Three trunked Beech tree, Conduit Wood

Opposite page:
Right: Veteran Oak
Far right: Browse line and deer guards
Top inset: Horse Chestnut buds

Veteran trees

The veteran trees are perhaps the Park's most outstanding feature. They are dotted throughout the parkland and woodlands and some are spaced in obvious lines, indicating very ancient field boundaries. Historically, many veteran trees were pollarded - a management technique where branches were cut above the grazing height of deer or cattle. This systematic way of producing timber started to decline in the late 18th century when we moved from wooden to steel ships. A better railway infrastructure brought alternative commodities to local communities and mechanisation favoured the production of timber from plantations. We stopped pollarding and started to closely plant trees in uniform rows to produce tall single-stemmed trees that were easier to mechanically harvest and process.

The veteran Oaks pre-date the enclosure of the Park and whilst we cannot be sure of their age, we can be confident that they are at least 500-700 years old. We know from historical records that funds were raised to repair the wall in 1659 'by felling and cutting of... pollards and under woods', so 350 years ago the trees must have been 150 - 350 years old. It also indicates that there were at least some areas of underwood in the Park - a layer of shrubby trees, most probably **Hazel** that would have been protected from the deer and managed for the products it supplied.

Establishing the age of veteran trees holds popular appeal, but it is really just an arbitrary number. Their significance lies in their condition and the habitats they support. The relative age of veteran trees also differs between species. It is for these reasons that the accepted definition of a veteran tree is: 'a tree that is of interest biologically, culturally or aesthetically because of its age, size or condition'. Of greatest significance is the number of trees the Park supports - offering continuity of habitats by having several specimens in close proximity to one another. Veteran and hollowing trees support abundant wildlife, associated with their decaying wood. In contrast, tall straight trees grown for sound timber are at an optimal stage for felling when they contain as much sound heartwood as possible - just before the decaying/hollowing process takes place.

Field Maples (just north of Isabella plantation), **Ash** (west of Prince Charles' Spinney), Hornbeam (south of Robin Hood Gate) and the very unusual **Black Poplar** (in the north of the Park). One of the Park's most notable veteran trees was the **Shrew Ash**, which under folk lore would cure ailments in children and cattle. What was left of this very old tree finally fell over in the 1987 storm and its location is now marked with a newly planted Ash.

There are around 1,000 veteran Oak trees across the whole Park, with good concentrations in High Wood and Queen Elizabeth Plantation. There are a few hundred veteran Hawthorns, with good examples to be found on the west facing slopes between Ham and Kingston Gates. Other veteran tree species include

Nowadays the veteran pollards have oversized, heavy limbs. It is possible to see where limbs have fallen off, often with detrimental effects on the longevity of the tree. Although they are no longer managed for timber production it is necessary to conserve them as cultural and biological assets. Arboriculture is the term used for the cultivation and management of trees. Veteran tree management is a branch of arboriculture that has attracted a great deal of development over the past 20 years. The Royal Parks is one of a number of organisations and companies that have developed the specialist techniques used to conserve veteran trees.

Above: Hollow Oak in High Wood
Below: Oak in 4 seasons

Woodlands

The density of tree cover varies across the Park but the distinction between woodland and parkland can be made if we assume woodland to be large areas of continuous canopy cover. They are well defined in Richmond Park as areas that were enclosed by a fence to protect a large number of trees from deer. In parkland, the low density of trees were given individual protection whilst the deer roamed amongst them. There are around 220 hectares of woodland in the Park and many of the mature woodlands are no longer enclosed. Those that are enclosed often provide the best sanctuary for wildlife, such as one plantation that supports a small breeding colony of Grey Herons, a bird that will not breed if it suffers even the slightest disturbance from people. The list of named woodlands is extensive, and their difference in character can be quite considerable. Many people form emotional attachments to woodlands and will have favourite areas of the Park, closely linked to the character and 'feel' that is created by dense tree cover.

Below: Three ages of Silver Birch
Top inset: Horse Chestnut bark
Right: Fencing protecting Coronation Plantation
Bottom right: Hornbeam walk

Many of the woodland blocks are around 200 years old and were planted under the management of Henry Addington, Viscount Sidmouth. In 1803 he was appointed as the Deputy Ranger and had accepted White Lodge as his residence. He undertook a systematic programme of plantations, and by the 1830s he had planted around 300 acres (120ha) of woodland including:

Sheen Wood, Sheen Cross Plantation, Spankers Hill Plantation, Sidmouth Wood, Pen Ponds Plantation, Ham Cross Wood, Roehampton Wood, Kingston Hill Wood, Kidney Wood and Conduit Wood.

Sidmouth would have selected species of trees to supply timber or bear large seeds that would feed the deer. In the early 18th century timber was a valuable commodity as world trade depended upon ships built from timber. Each ship would require around 3,000 trees, requiring 50 acres (20ha) of mature Oak woodland. Richmond Park followed the national trend to create woodlands, but by the late 18th century ship building favoured steel and the management of Oak woodland became less profitable - sparing the Richmond Park woodlands from the axe. These 200-year-old trees can be found as tall, single stemmed mature trees that are starting to show signs of age. They are just beyond optimum timber yield and they have started to undergo the natural processes that produce dead wood and hollowing not offered by younger trees. As such they are starting to offer the essential continuity of habitat to all the specialist wildlife supported by the veteran Oak trees.

Ancient woodland is a term given to areas that have been continuously wooded since at least 1600. As with most of Greater London, there are no areas of the Park on the official ancient woodland inventory. Historic records, a series of maps and signs on the ground, indicate that Prince Charles' Spinney and parts of Isabella Plantation are long established woodlands, and probably ancient.

In particular the populations of Bluebells and 'standard' veteran trees (not pollarded) indicate that these areas once supported an under-wood. This lower canopy of woodland comprised multi stemmed shrub forming species - commonly **Hazel**. Under-wood was cut on a rotational basis, the hazel stools quickly re-growing a crop of straight rods every 5 to 10 years or so. The dynamic structure of coppice woodlands provides recently cut, new and mature growth - which in turn supports a variety of wildlife that enjoys sunlit woodland, dense impenetrable growth and mature shrubs. Isabella Plantation is now managed as a world class woodland garden, but Prince Charles' Spinney has undergone a variety of management objectives over many years. It has an eclectic mix of non-native species and poor woodland structure. In 2008 a programme of work started to restore the woodland back to coppice woodland and regain the benefits this will offer to wildlife.

This page:
Top: Tercentenary Plantation of Beech

Opposite page:
Right: Lime - an unusual species in the Park
Far right above: Woodpecker holes in Silver Birch and Rhododendron on Pen Ponds
Bottom right: Rhododendron undergrowth in Isabella Plantation
Top inset: Rhododendron

Scrub

Like under-woods, scrub habitats provide a lower layer of vegetation which has an important role in the landscape and ecosystem. It provides cover for birds and its nectar, seeds and berries provide food for all, including insects. Patches of **Gorse** and Hawthorn around Conduit Wood have been protected from deer browsing and now support a particular group of song birds including Whitethroats, Blackcaps and other warblers. Small islands of scrub, situated in grassland, make the best habitat for birds. They like to nest in the safety of the scrub and feed in the grassland around them - gaining the 'bed-and-breakfast' they need whilst they stay to breed in the summer months.

Elsewhere deer are excluded from woodland areas. Two Storm Wood, Sidmouth Wood and other smaller enclosures all provide a valuable shrub layer, supporting birds and other wildlife not found in the parkland.

Rhododendron

Rhododendron is an introduced shrub that is native to Asia and southern Europe. The Victorians valued rhododendron for ornament and game cover, but today it is regarded by many as invasive and damaging to habitats. It is unpalatable, even to deer, and its branches grow randomly. Where they touch the ground it readily roots and continues to spread vegetatively until it dominates and displaces all other species.

Although it supports little insect life and offers little to the ecosystem, Rhododendron does offer some physical cover for deer and is retained in a few areas for them. It also creates an atmospheric walk for anyone taking the shortcut through the Driftway in Sidmouth Woods.

Riparian woodland

Some tree species are especially suited to growing in wet soil, close to rivers and ponds or on low-lying areas prone to waterlogging and floods. The Beverly Brook is lined with over 100 **Crack Willows** and a few **Weeping Willows**. The name Crack Willow indicates the brittle nature of the weak timber and the tree's tendency to collapse. However, the fallen branches take root and re-grow quickly, a characteristic that allowed Crack Willow to flourish in the distant past when untamed rivers scoured out riverbanks during winter floods. The Crack Willows along the Beverly Brook are now pollarded on a cyclical basis to prevent them from falling in, but a few veteran trees can be seen east of Cambrian Gate. A few Alders can be found at Ham Gate Pond, Adam's Pond and Pen Ponds. As with all riparian trees, Alders grow very quickly and produce low density timber that ignites easily but burns out quickly. This property makes for poor quality firewood, but once made into charcoal, Alder was the tree of choice for making gunpowder.

The Park is also proud to host a small number of mature Black Poplars. It is thought that there are only around 8,000 mature Black Poplars in the UK (to put that in context - Richmond Park alone has almost 60,000 Oaks). Its rarity has attracted the efforts of conservation bodies and new trees are being planted through a number of programmes that include one in Richmond and the surrounding area.

Ornamental plantings and feature trees

Within the parkland and woodland are a number of unusual trees, presumably planted for ornament and interest for the Park visitor. The history of some of these trees is known, for example the Sugar Maples near Kingston Gate, planted in recognition of the Canadian support in World War II. The avenue of Hornbeams south of Pembroke Lodge was obviously planted to line the path running south. Elsewhere **Monkey Puzzle, Holm Oaks** and Cedars can be found in locations that make them visible and are there to be enjoyed. Other trees seem to be in obscure places, possibly just planted in with the mix of general trees or possibly left over from planting schemes in the formal gardens and deemed 'too good to waste'. It is a worthwhile challenge to try to find the **Cork Oaks** in Coronation Plantation or the **Handkerchief Tree** in Prince Charles' Spinney.

Above right: Bark of the Cork Oak
Right: Handkerchief tree

Management today

The Park has little room for any new large scale plantations, but tree planting continues to maintain continuity of woodland areas and replace lost trees. Where an opportunity arises, the occasional feature tree is planted in parkland areas, but these are limited as we need to resist crowding the trees and restricting crown growth. Transplanting trees is stressful. They cope better when very small and a proportionately larger root system can be easily lifted. However, trees in Richmond Park need to be around six to eight feet tall (2.5m) to be above the height of grazing deer, and so the relatively small root system is inevitably reduced a little when lifted from the nursery. Trees are planted in winter when dormant and, provided the following summer is not too dry, tend to establish well.

The health of the Park's trees varies between species and the evidence is clear that some are not faring very well. All mature **Elms** were lost in the Park when nationally they were ravaged in the late 20th century by Dutch elm disease. Elms do survive in the Park but only as 'suckers' - young growth from underground roots. But once they get to vulnerable size, they too will be lost and constantly replaced by new suckers. Dutch elm disease was a single pathogen which all but wiped out the species. Most trees tend to suffer from a modern unhealthy lifestyle. The compound effects of air pollution, climate change, root compaction, pathogens such as mildew and non-native insects, squirrel and bird damage all take their toll. Of particular concern are the Horse Chestnuts and **English Oaks.** They are surviving in Richmond Park and some are still flourishing, but the number of trees with poor growth and sparse crowns is a concern to all tree lovers.

Active management of the trees is a combination of work intended to help safeguard the longevity of trees or 'managed-decline' where the trees are safely dismantled to reduce the risk of collapse on the many Park visitors. With Richmond Park receiving more visitors than any of the other 224 National Nature Reserves and with so many trees, there is always a lot to do.

The trees in the Park will always survive although the composition of species, and variation in cover may alter a little over time. The quintessential image of the city skyline set in the juxtaposition of the tree tops is safe. Each human generation has good intent when they claim to manage this landscape, but trees are long-lived and their presence is humbling. Woodland colour illuminates the changing seasons and creates a year-round rhythm for the daily visitor. Trees offer us a sense of reliability and permanence that has become increasingly difficult to find in modern city life. As W. H. Auden wrote, *'A culture is no better than its woods'.*

Top inset: Maple, new growth
Below: Tercentenary Wood

Flora

By Jacqueline Shane, Richmond Park Flora Group.

Richmond Park is not renowned for its flora but, if you know where to look, the Park has some surprising and subtle gems, particularly the mosaic of plants associated with the predominantly acid soil. The majority of plants described are native to the British Isles and have arrived in the Park unaided. So far, over 450 species have been recorded.

Mid Spring

A good time to start botanising: **Lords and Ladies** or **Cuckoo-Pint** appear along the Park walls; a strange flower comprising a spike enclosed in a sheath and designed to attract and then trap flies - for a short period - to aid pollination. Later on the plant will produce its characteristic cluster of red berries. **Good Friday Grass**, not actually a grass but a low growing **Wood-Rush**, with conspicuous bright yellow anthers (the pollen-producing part of the flower) starts to appear in quantity generally around Easter time. Look now for **Common Dog-Violet**, sometimes attractively combined with **Lesser Celandine**, a low-growing member of the butter-cup family, in areas of short grass which can be found just outside the lower, western end of Prince Charles' Spinney. **Toad Rush**, generally a small, and often very small, tufted rush, common in the Park, will appear alongside many paths where, being an annual, it can exploit bare ground.

Opposite page: English Bluebells

This page:
Above right: Common Dog Violets
Right: Lords and Ladies, with cluster of red berries
Top inset: Good Friday Grass (Field Wood-Rush)

Late Spring

A period when the Park shows us some of its specialities and even rarities. **English Bluebells** are apparent at this time, often growing amongst bracken, but also in some quantity in Isabella Plantation. Unfortunately, English Bluebells have been hybridising for some years with the introduced **Spanish Bluebell**. These hybrids are certainly present in the Park, particularly round the perimeter and even in Prince Charles' Spinney. Now is the time to seek out **Heath Dog-Violet**, quite similar to Common Dog-Violet but with a later flowering period. One way to distinguish it from Common Dog-Violet is by its leaves, which are more oval and do not form a basal rosette. This is not a common plant and is one of the Park's specialities which can be found adjoining the south-eastern bank of Ham Cross Ditch. Also, in and near this ditch, you should find **Heath Milkwort**, a low plant with delicate, generally blue or pink flowers.

Two more of the Park's specialities, often associated with acid soils, will now begin to appear on and amongst anthills in comparatively short grassland: **Heath Speedwell**, with a spike of mid-blue flowers, and **Sheep's Sorrel,** a diminutive version of sorrel with a red flower stalk imparting a reddish hue to whole patches. Now is your chance to get to know some grasses with a couple of early flowering species: **Sweet Vernal-Grass,** low growing with a spike-like inflorescence (flower), sweet smelling like hay when crushed, and **Meadow Foxtail**, a tallish grass, resembling its name with its cylindrical inflorescence.

This page:
Below left: Sheep's Sorrel
Below right: Heath Speedwell

Opposite page:
Below left: Mouse-ear Hawkweed
Below right: Tormentil
Top inset: Lady's Bedstraw

Early Summer

Everything is rushing into flower: **Cow Parsley**; **Foxglove**; members of the **Pea Family (Common Bird's-Foot Trefoil** - the seed head resembles a Bird's foot - **Common Vetch, Meadow Vetchling,** and **Grass Vetchling** - the leaves really are grass-like, but look for the crimson flowers); **Lesser** and **Greater Stitchwort** with delicate white flowers; **Hairy Sedge,** probably the most common sedge in the Park, low growing with brownish male flowers at the tip above several thicker greenish female ones - the leaves are indeed hairy; **Goat's-Beard** or **Jack-Go-To -Bed-At-Noon** - the yellow dandelion-like flowers actually close up at noon - notable for its impressive 'clock' seed head; **Cat's-Ear,** another dandelion-like flower on a leafless flower stem. **Heath Bedstraw** with its clusters of tiny white flowers; **Mouse-Ear Hawkweed** with vibrant lemon yellow dandelion-like flowers; and **Tormentil,** low-growing with yellow flowers of, usually, four petals, now join with the other flowers of acid grassland to show us nature's version of the medieval 'Enamelled Mead'.

In good years, the area south of the restricted road that runs from Ham Cross to the Pen Ponds car park and west of the car park can be out-standing. Also, the areas west of Sidmouth Wood and between the road to Richmond Gate and Bishop's Pond will be worth visiting. Incidentally, Hawkweeds, it is said, are so named because Dioscorides, a first century Greek physician and botanist, thought that hawks used these plants in some way to aid their sight. Some typical and common rushes to look out for are: **Hard, Soft & Compact,** with their inflorescences apparently on the side of the flowering stem. The grey-green stems of Hard Rush have easily felt ridges, whereas the greener stems of Soft Rush will feel smooth. And, **Slender Rush** with greenish inflorescence nestling amongst apparent leaves, is much in evidence along damp tracks, especially near the Park wall.

The majority of grasses now come into flower: look for **Wavy Hair-Grass,** an attractive short grass with a graceful silvery open inflorescence, common throughout the Park and indicative of Acid Grassland, as also is **Tufted Hair-Grass,** a tall, tufted, grass with a feathery inflorescence, in damper areas and very common; **Wall Barley,** a generally short grass with long whiskers - often seen growing by the road-side and at the base of walls; and **Mat-Grass,** a low, small tufted grass with a one-sided inflorescent spike. The last-named is a grass that is normally found in upland moorland areas, so rather unusual in Greater London and a speciality of the Park. A good place to spot this grass is along the wide path north of Sidmouth Wood leading to Pen Ponds. And look now for the bright yellow fragrant flower clusters of **Lady's Bedstraw,** said to have been used to scent straw mattresses and, possibly, ward off undesirable insects. It is fairly common in the Park, and found in quantity at Ham Bottom.

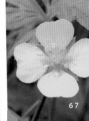

Many plants from early summer will still be in flower, but there will be some additions. **Common Ragwort** with clusters of yellow daisy-like flowers is a somewhat maligned plant, but it is the food-plant of the Cinnabar Moth. Unfortunately, it is also poisonous to livestock, but not deer, especially when dried in hay. **Autumn Hawkbit,** another dandelion-like flower and easy to confuse with Cat's-Ear, but having branched flower stems and leaves more like those of dandelions, will begin to appear and carry on until well into autumn.

Purple Moor Grass, a tall, tussocky grass, can be found in damp places with purple inflorescence. As its name implies, this grass is typical of acidic moorland and fairly common in the Park; there is a particularly extensive area just outside Isabella Plantation on the north side. And, finally, for this period, look for the charming **Harebell** with its delicate, mauvy-blue flowers. It pops up here and there, but one reliable area is by the water covers near Kidney Wood. Harebells are not specific to acid grassland and, indeed, are probably more abundant in chalk grassland. But we are lucky to have this delightful flower in Richmond Park and it has been deemed a flagship plant for the Park.

This page:
Left: Common Ragwort
Below left: Harebell
Below right: Purple Moor Grass

Opposite page:
Below far right: Skullcap
Below left: Lady's Smock
Top inset: Water Figwort

Wetland plants found by the edges of ponds, streams and ditches

Mid to late Spring: look for **Cuckoo Flower** or **Lady's Smock** with attractive lilac or pink flowers. If you are very lucky you may even hear a cuckoo with which this plant's flowering is said to be associated. Look for this on the banks of Bishop's Pond, where later on you should see **Water Forget-Me-Not** (also around the edges of Upper and Lower Pen Ponds).

Early summer: **Lesser Spearwort**, a member of the buttercup family, growing in the margins of White Ash Pond and Lower Pen Pond; **Skullcap**, with bright blue-lipped flowers, by Lower and Upper Pen Ponds, also Ham Dip pond; **Brooklime**, a speedwell with the customary blue flowers that likes to grow in damp places - Ham Cross ditch; **Water Figwort** - fig being an old name for piles, which it was thought parts of the plant resembled, and for which Figwort was a medieval remedy - edge of Conduit Stream and other wet places.

Mid Summer: **Water Mint** is an attractive addition to this period with its rounded lilac-coloured flowerheads - margins of Upper and Lower Pen Ponds.

Late Summer is the time for **Common Reed**, a very tall grass, to show its graceful spreading browny-purplish inflorescence. It can be seen to great effect in Upper Pen Pond, together with another component of a reedbed, namely **Bulrush,** with its characteristic stout brown cylindrical flower, the female part; and the slimmer, yellowish male flower above. As it is not, in fact, a rush, many books have attempted to wean us off this 'incorrect' name and it is also called **Common Reedmace.**

Finally, some plants with floating or submerged leaves to look for: **Starworts,** with a star-like rosette of small leaves in ponds, streams and ditches, often on mud; **Duckweeds,** forming a floating mat of very small apparent leaves; **Pondweeds,** quite a large plant family with a range of leaf shapes and sizes. **Broad-leaved Pondweed** with broad oval leaves is probably one of the easiest to recognise - Upper Pen Pond, Ham Cross Pond and the Beverley Brook.

Garden areas

By Jo Scrivener, Assistant Park Manager.

Richmond Park has two main garden areas. Pembroke Lodge Gardens is a more formal garden, originally laid out 150 years ago. Isabella Plantation is an informal woodland garden developed 50 years ago within a Victorian plantation. Both gardens offer a rich and colourful mix of plants and trees, with something to see year round.

Pembroke Lodge Gardens

Pembroke Lodge Gardens occupy an area of 11 acres (4.5ha), situated on the western side of the Park, to the south of Richmond Gate. The Lodge and its surrounding Gardens sit on an escarpment which offers panoramic views across the Thames Valley. Pembroke Lodge dates back largely to the 18th century and today houses a public restaurant and private functions business.

Originally known as Hill Lodge and marked on old maps as the 'Mole Catchers Cottage', the Lodge was altered and extended by the famous architect Sir John Soane for the Countess Elizabeth of Pembroke in the 1780s and 1790s. The Countess resided in the Lodge until her death in 1831.

Lord John Russell, the Victorian Prime Minister, was granted tenure by Queen Victoria in 1847 and occupied the Lodge from then until 1878. Lord John was responsible for much of the garden's current layout. The garden he created was essentially a woodland garden with ancient oaks and shaded lawns containing carpets of Bluebells and Daffodils, which still flower today throughout the spring. Bertrand Russell, the philosopher and grandson of Lord John, spent his childhood years at Pembroke Lodge and in his memoirs describes many fine trees including Cedar of Lebanon and Japanese Cedars, as well as Sweet Briar hedges and summer houses. He also mentions several formal flower gardens with Box hedges. However he does state that the gardens fell into decline during his grandparents' later years.

The more formal or designed elements of the garden are relatively recent with the majority occurring in the last century when Pembroke Lodge was opened as public tea rooms. Additions of the time included a new approach to the front of the Lodge, from a new car park, and the paved terraces to the rear of the building.

The gardens are currently undergoing another period of change, which began in 1997 with the removal of the Dahlia borders situated on the eastern boundary of the Garden either side of the main entrance. This area was replaced with a mixed border with shrubs to provide structure and year round interest, and herbaceous perennials and bulbs to provide spring and summer interest. Plants of interest in this bed include the **Mimosa** or **Silver Wattle**, a small tree with silver green divided leaves that produces an abundance of fragrant yellow flowers in late winter/early spring. Also the **Foxglove Tree**, which when cut back to a framework in late winter produces a mass of very large leaves.

As well as seeking to improve the gardens with new plantings many traditional elements of horticulture remain. Seasonal bedding is planted in the South Bed (at the south end of the Lodge), Terrace Beds (west terrace to the rear of the Lodge), Centre Beds (north of the Rose Garden) and also at Poets' Corner (north of King Henry's Mound). Bedding is a Park tradition dating back to the Victorian era and has been present within the Park since the post war years. Schemes are planted twice a year to provide colour throughout the winter/spring (planted October) and summer months (planted mid-May).

In 2003 the reception area at the front of the Lodge was formalised and the building framed with box parterre hedging containing knots of **Lavender** and **Silver Bush**, York stone paving and herbaceous borders. **London Plane** trees were also added to the rear terrace and 'pleached' (the art of training trees into a raised hedge) to provide shade for alfresco diners. A gravel garden was also added to a sunken area adjoining the north end of the Lodge to soften the building. Plants here are grown for their architectural interest and include many contrasting leaf shapes; tree ferns grow alongside bamboo and ornamental grasses to provide dramatic effect.

In addition to this, at the south end of the gardens in the Dell area, a series of informal paths and beds have been planted with specimen trees, shrubs and woodland shade perennials which are at their peak of flower in the spring. A number of shrubs provide interest throughout the autumn and winter months and include the **Cornelian Cherry** and **Witch Hazel**.

Previous page:
Main picture: Seasonal bedding, Pembroke Lodge, south border
Top inset: Children's entertainment

This page:
Above left: Russian Sage and Yarrow
Below: Dahlias and Lantana

Opposite page:
Top inset: Angel's trumpet, seasonal bedding

Although bedding is a traditional practice, today the aim is to make it more sustainable. Since 2004 all the Park's seasonal bedding is grown in peat-free composts to help prevent the further destruction of peat bog habitat. Beds are also single dug on a rotational basis and mulch (produced locally from composted garden soft plant materials, chipped woody prunings and horse manure) is incorporated into beds. This not only provides valuable nutrients for plants, but is also moisture retentive, thus reducing the need for excessive watering during the hot summer months. Today many of the plants used within bedding schemes will be used again. Herbaceous perennials and shrubs have been added into the mix of annuals and half hardy annuals, with plants selected so that they can be reused in this and other garden areas within the Park.

The gardens also house a number of plant collections. Originally a bowling green in Lord John Russell's time, the Rose Garden is now home to a collection of **Floribunda** and **Hybrid Tea** roses which are at their peak of flower in the summer months. The Lissaman Iris Collection is planted in the west facing bed adjacent to the historic herringbone brick wall at Poets' Corner. This collection is predominately made up of **Tall Bearded Iris**, which are mainly American cultivars from the 1960s and 1970s. This collection was gifted to the Park in the 1990s by a local nurseryman and collector, George Lissaman. Bearded Iris flower from late May to mid-June and colours range from rich mahogany reds through to pale blues. The collection remained behind the scenes until 2003 when renaming began.

There are currently in excess of 30 named cultivars with many plants waiting to be identified behind the scenes in the Gardens' nursery stock beds.

Situated between the Rose Garden and Poets' Corner is King Henry's Mound, the Gardens' most important historical landscape feature. It is believed to be an ancient Bronze Age barrow and the site where Henry VIII watched the deer during a hunt. Look to the east from the Mound to see the vista to St Paul's Cathedral and to the west for a stunning panoramic view of Surrey and beyond.

The John Beer Laburnum Arch links Poets' Corner to King Henry's Mound and is named after a former chargehand of the Gardens. **Laburnums** are pruned annually in late winter before the sap rises. The main leaders are tied in and tipped to encourage lateral growth and the laterals are then spur pruned to two or three buds. The arch produces an abundance of beautiful drooping pea-like yellow flowers in May.

In addition the Gardens have a broad range of interesting trees and shrubs. The perimeter shelter belts are planted with old hardy hybrid **Rhododendrons** and **Camellia** cultivars which flower through the spring and summer months. The Lawns to the south and north of the Lodge have in excess of 15 ancient **Pedunculate** or common **Oaks**. These trees are mainly lapsed pollards, originally cut to a height of 2.5 - 3m and harvested for wood, and are a characteristic feature of the gardens and the Park.

Many interesting trees are grown within the Gardens. **Catalpa fargesii** grows on the lawn to the east of the Laburnum Arch and is a smaller leaved relative of the **Indian Bean Tree**. It produces rose pink panicles of flowers in June followed by long slender seed pods.

At the north end of the Lodge opposite the front lawns on a small mound grows the **Golden Rain Tree**. This tree has deeply-lobed spreading leaves and yellow flowers in summer followed by lantern shaped fruits.

The **Bull Bay** grows in the recesses on the west side of the house. This small tree is kept in check by pruning. It has evergreen glossy leaves with a reddish brown velvety underside and produces very large fragrant cream flowers in late summer and early autumn.

The **Persian Ironwood** grows on the edge of the meadow lawn below the rear terrace. This small tree with its spreading shape has flecked bark similar to that of the London Plane. In autumn its leaves turn yellow to crimson and in March it produces small red flowers on its stems.

The **Paperbark Maple** on the South Lawn not only produces reddish-orange autumn colour on its leaves but also paper-like shedding bark. A **Snakebark Maple** also grows on the South Lawn; it is a native of Asia and is olive green in colour in almost all its parts, from leaves and shoots to flowers. This maple shows good rich orange to dark red autumn colour; however, it is primarily grown for the snake-like appearance of its bark, which is its best feature.

Previous page:
Top: Mixed borders provide year round interest
Below right: Bedding display

This page:
Below: Summer bedding - centre beds
Top inset: Centre beds with views west

South of the Lodge on the banks to the Dell, adjacent to the steps, is a stand of **Tibetan Cherries** grown for their shedding translucent bark which takes on fiery hues when lit up by sunlight. Further south on this bank is the **Handkerchief Tree**. Its name derives from the small flower heads that appear in May surrounded by attractive large white handkerchief-like bracts.

The **Coast Redwood** stands in the Dell on the south west side of the Gardens bounding Petersham Park. This American conifer grows to be one of the tallest trees in the world and has a stunning rust coloured bark. Growing next to the Coast Redwood is the **Swamp Cypress** another American native conifer which grows in tidal creeks and absorbs oxygen from the air by sending up knee-like growths (pneumataphores) from its roots. This tree is a deciduous conifer with leaves that turn orangey-red in autumn before shedding.

75

The Bog Garden in Spring
Top inset: Streamside paths

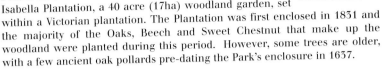

Isabella Plantation

Found in the centre of the Park, east of Ham Cross, is Isabella Plantation, a 40 acre (17ha) woodland garden, set within a Victorian plantation. The Plantation was first enclosed in 1831 and the majority of the Oaks, Beech and Sweet Chestnut that make up the woodland were planted during this period. However, some trees are older, with a few ancient oak pollards pre-dating the Park's enclosure in 1637.

The name Isabella Plantation is thought to have been derived from old English. Historic maps of the Park mark this area as 'Isabell Slade'. Isabell is thought to mean dingy yellow (possibly referring to the colour of the topsoil in some areas of the garden), and Slade is a term for a shallow valley.

Work on the gardens began in the late 1940s and they were first opened to the public in 1953. The gardens have developed from a simple streamside walk to a large collection of woodland trees and shrubs surrounding three inter-connecting ponds and four streams. Today the gardens' ponds and streams are fed by water pumped from Pen Ponds (large ponds situated in the centre of the Park) and pumped via a series of pipes and ditches to the top of the Plantation and then returned back to Pen Ponds via an outlet from Peg's Pond. Much of the Garden layout seen today was developed by George Thomson (a former Park Superintendent) and his head gardener, Wally Miller. Their philosophy for the gardens has been further developed by a dedicated garden team and subsequent Park managers.

The shady conditions and acidic sandy soils provide ideal conditions for a wide range of woodland trees and shrubs including **Rhododendron ponticum** (an invasive exotic in many woodlands), which is managed by pruning and provides an evergreen backdrop to the Plantation's main collections.

The Gardens are perhaps best known for the evergreen **Azaleas** that line the ponds and streams and are at their peak of flower in late April and early May. In addition to this, the Plantation houses the National Collection of Wilson 50 **Kurume Azaleas**, collected by the famous plant hunter Ernest Wilson in Japan in the 1920s. The gardens also contain large and important collections of old hardy hybrid Rhododendron and species Rhododendron, as well as large collections of **Camellia japonica** cultivars and a broad range of rare and unusual trees and shrubs.

Today Isabella Plantation is classified as part of the broader parkland Site of Special Scientific Interest (SSSI). The gardens are managed organically, very much with nature in mind and without recourse to the use of pesticides or herbicides. Leaf mould is collected and composted for use as a surface mulch and soil conditioner. Park bracken is also used as a peat substitute and is cut annually and composted for use as an acid compost, mulch and soil conditioner for Rhododendrons and other acid loving plants.

The gardens offer something to see all year round. One of the first signs of spring is the yellow spathes of the **Skunk Cabbage** which line the Plantation's streams. In spring the gardens' collection of Camellias and **Magnolias** bloom.

Bulbs such as native **Daffodils** begin flowering and are followed by **Bluebells** which flower in naturalised drifts around the garden. Rhododendron and Azalea flower from the early spring and throughout the summer months.

In summer, **Day Lilies** and **Candelabra Primulas** also flower in the Bog Garden. In late summer the white panicles of the **Oak-Leaved Hydrangeas** flower in various areas of the garden, and the blue flower spikes of **Pickerel Weed** flower in the gardens' ponds and pools.

Clockwise from top left:
Summer flowering deciduous Azaleas,
Snowdrop tree, Evergreen Azaleas,
Tupelo tree at Thompson's Pond,
Snakes head Fritillary, Asian Skunk
Cabbage, Camellia sasanqua.

the autumn the gardens are alive with colours which range from rich reds and scarlets through to oranges and butter yellows. Trees which provide autumn leaf colour include Maples, **Sweet Gum, Black Gum** or **Tupelo trees, Tulip trees** and the Persian Ironwood. Deciduous conifers such as the Swamp Cypress and the Dawn Redwood add fiery crowns and orange hues to the gardens' autumnal palette of colours. Many of the gardens' shrubs also bear bright autumn fruits such as the **Guelder Rose, Spindle, Rowan and Hawthorn.**

In winter the Plantation's cold air is warmed by the scents of **Winter Flowering Honeysuckle, Oregon Grape, Wintersweet** and Witch Hazels.

At this time of year the decorative and colourful barks of trees such as the Tibetan Cherry and the Paperbark Maple are also more obvious.

Throughout the gardens native plants can be found growing alongside more exotic introductions. Areas such as the Heather garden with its collection of **Erica** and **Calluna** cultivars aim to mimic natural heathland. Heathers are allowed to grow without excessive pruning and are planted alongside native shrubs associated with wild heathland, such as **Gorse**, native **Broom** and **Tree Heaths**, which also provide additional height, colour and texture to the display.

Above: Acers provide Autumn colour

Top inset: Tulip tree in Autumn
Above: Winter flowering Witch Hazel
Below: Azalea display at the Still Pond in May

The Bog Garden with its series of interconnecting pools is planted with a wide range of exotic marginals such as **Elephant Rhubarb**, and ornamental grasses such as **Golden Oats**. These plants grow alongside native perennials such as **Purple Loosestrife, Joe Pye Weed, Rosebay Willow Herb** and **Meadowsweet**, and shrubs such as **Dogwood** and pollarded **Willow**, which produce coloured stems in winter.

The gardens are surrounded by a conservation area which is not open to the public and provides a safe refuge for wildlife. The perimeter shelterbelts of the garden are planted with native nectar and berry bearing shrubs. **Wild Bramble** and **Stinging Nettle** are also allowed to colonise these areas to provide additional food and shelter for birds and insects.

Top: The Bog Garden in summer,
Above right: Streamside marginals,
Middle: Royal Fern along streams,
Below right: Summer flowering
Pickerel weed

The gardens' many and varied habitats support a broad range of wildlife. Foxes and Badgers find shelter in the fringes of the garden and its conservation area.

The Plantation's ponds are home to a wide range of birds including Mallards, Coots and Moorhen as well as wildfowl including Tufted Duck, Pochard, Shelduck and Mandarin. Heron also fish in the gardens' ponds and streams. Dragonflies, Damselflies, frogs, toads and grass snakes breed and feed in the Plantation's waters.

The gardens trees and shrubs attract many birds for food and shelter including Blackbirds, Thrushes, Robins as well as Willow Warbler, Chiffchaff and Blackcap and Green and Greater Spotted Woodpecker, which can often be heard drumming in the trees.

The mix of native and exotic planting includes native perennials, which provide a valuable source of nectar for a wide range of insects including bees, wasps, butterflies and moths. These attractive plants are retained in areas such as the Bog Garden and along sections of stream; their spread is controlled by the removal of flower heads prior to seeding.

The Plantation is also home to a large population of ancient trees including native Common or Pedunculate Oak, Beech and Hornbeam which are high in biodiversity and have their own associated ecosystems. In order to protect species and habitat wherever possible, dead wood is retained in gardens, for the benefit of a wide range of wildlife including birds, bats, wood-rotting fungi and dead-wood invertebrates. It also adds aesthetic and historic value to the Plantation. Decaying wood is retained as standing deadwood in the form of monoliths (dead trees with reduced branches), and as stumps or fallen logs in the form of bird tables and seats.

Above: Oak-Leaved Hydrangea
Right: Native flora
Top inset: Katsura tree in autumn colour

Above: *Veteran oaks marking the pre-enclosure boundary of Hill Farm*
Below: *Enclosure map of 1637*
Top inset: *A section of the old wall*

KEY

Roads
Manor boundaries
(including sub-divisions
of Wimbledon Manor)
Dwelling houses

Place names and descriptions are shown
in capitals

Owners of land aquired directly (or through
Viscount Wimbledon) are not bracketed.
Owners of land aquired through Earl of
Portland or Kingston Borough are bracketed

RICHMOND
PETERSHAM
RICHMOND
COMMON
PETERSHAM MANOR HOUSE
WHITE CONDUIT
LITTLE HEATH COMMON
HILL FARM
MORTLAKE
BERRY GROVE
PETERSHAM COMMON
MORTLAKE GREAT HEATH COMMON
MORTLAKE SOUTH COMMON FIELD
ASHEN CLOSE PALE COMMON
THE SUDBROOK
HAM
WOODS
HAM
HAM COMMON
WOODS
WOODS NEW GATE WOODS
SHEEP HAWE
LOANES
RUT-NELLS
SLAWOOD
SIXTEEN ACRES
HARTLETON HILL WOOD
LAMBERT HAWES
LORD COPE
HARTLE-TON FARM
DUNDIDGE GROUNDS
BLACK HEATH
HALARS GROVE
HYE FIELDS
BEVERLEY MEADS
BEVERLEY CLOSES
KINGSTON NORTH FIELD
BEVERLEY PLAIN
KINGSTON
PUTNEY
COMMON
PUTNEY

furlongs
half-mile

82

History
By Max Lankester, Secretary, Friends of Richmond Park

Without the selfish and unpopular actions of one man in the 1630s, the space we cherish as Richmond Park would probably be just another stretch of suburbia. With the passage of time, an enclosure that was once bitterly resented has become a cause for celebration.

King Charles I was said to be 'extremely partial to the sports of the chase'. His passion for hunting, coupled with his autocratic approach to his role as monarch and his belief in the 'divine right of kings', led him to establish his 'New Park' in Richmond. (It bore that name to distinguish it from what is now known as the Old Deer Park between Richmond and Kew.) He could have created a hunting park anywhere, but Richmond had the advantage of being close to London, and it was an area already well known to the King. He had been brought up at Richmond Palace as a child, and in 1617 it had become his official residence as Prince of Wales. In 1627 he settled the Palace on his new Queen, Henrietta Maria, to be in turn a house for their children.

The area which Charles chose to requisition is shown on the 1637 map opposite. It was much like any area of land around which one might construct an eight-mile wall, and contained roads, farms and common land as well as certain woods and other areas already in the King's ownership. Because of the existence of the commons, over which the inhabitants of various parishes had historic rights, and because there were private houses and lands within the area coveted by the King, he found the acquisition 'a work of some difficulty'. Some of Charles' advisers cautioned against such an expensive and unpopular project. The King, however, was not to be dissuaded, and proceeded to have the bricks manufactured for the wall.

Although the King's officials offered more than the value of the various landholdings, and many of the owners consented to part with their lands to oblige him, others could not be prevailed on to sell on any terms. So Charles simply started to have the wall built on his own lands, which concentrated the minds of some waverers. Many who agreed to sell resented the compulsory nature of the transaction. The people of Mortlake were particularly put out by the loss of a large part of their common lands, and the Mortlake Vestry received no compensation for land taken by the King. The wall was completed in 1637 and Jerome, Earl of Portland, was made the first Keeper in 1638.

From the outset, Charles permitted people to come into the Park to gather firewood; he also kept the roads across the Park open to pedestrians. These concessions were probably an attempt to retain some measure of popularity rather than a genuine wish to preserve the established rights of his subjects. Having risked so much on its creation, Charles had only a short time to enjoy hunting in his New Park, since by 1642 Civil War was raging. He nevertheless hunted when he could, and was even allowed to make what was probably his last visit to the Park in August 1647 while he was a prisoner at Hampton Court, less than 18 months before his execution in January 1649.

The Civil War

After Charles I's execution on 30 January 1649, Parliament abolished the monarchy and Cromwell declared the start of the Commonwealth. Richmond Park was clearly no longer a Royal Park. On 17 July 1649 the House of Commons passed an Act for settling the Park on the Mayor, Commonalty and Citizens of London (i.e. the City Corporation) and their Successors forever. This followed swiftly after the Corporation had lavishly entertained the Commons to a dinner in the City. The Commons expressed the wish that *'the keepers in the new Park be continued in their respective places, and enjoy the profits thereunto belonging, they continuing faithful to their trust'*.

For the next 11 years the Park was under the stewardship of the City, which spent considerable sums on the deer and on repairing the wall. The Park did produce an income, however, through the sale of timber.

As soon as it was clear that the monarchy would be restored, the City Corporation was quick to curry favour with the new King. Even before Charles II had set sail for England, the Corporation sent a deputation to meet him in The Hague; they gave him £10,000 and promised that the Park would be restored to him. Within days of Charles' triumphal entry into London on 29 May 1660, the Recorder reported on 2 June that *'himself and the Rt Hon Lord Mayor, together with the Aldermen, had this afternoon attended his Majesty in order to congratulate his Majesty's Restoration and likewise to present the Newe Parke to his Majesty; and that he (the Lord Mayor) did declare that it was done by way of restitution and not gift; and further said it was well it was in the City's hands for that they had preserved the wood ... and game'*.

The record continues that *'His Majesty returned answer that the City of London were still loading him with their kindness and that he looked upon the said Park to be kept for him and that he accepted it not as restored but as freely given unto him by the City and thanked them for the same'*. The new King was as adept at insincere flattery as the Corporation!

Below: Beating the Bounds 1751, led by the Vicar of Richmond

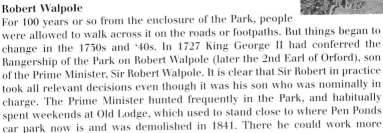

Public Access to the Park

Robert Walpole

For 100 years or so from the enclosure of the Park, people were allowed to walk across it on the roads or footpaths. But things began to change in the 1730s and '40s. In 1727 King George II had conferred the Rangership of the Park on Robert Walpole (later the 2nd Earl of Orford), son of the Prime Minister, Sir Robert Walpole. It is clear that Sir Robert in practice took all relevant decisions even though it was his son who was nominally in charge. The Prime Minister hunted frequently in the Park, and habitually spent weekends at Old Lodge, which used to stand close to where Pen Ponds car park now is and was demolished in 1841. There he could work more effectively than in central London.

Sir Robert and George II would often hunt together, typically on Wednesdays and Saturdays. They would have used White Lodge (formerly known as New Lodge), which had been commissioned by George I and completed in 1729 for his successor. Sir Robert had expended large sums on Old Lodge, Thatched House Lodge and on other improvements. Because of that expenditure and his wish to hunt in privacy, Sir Robert built keepers' lodges at the gates; at the same time he removed the ladder stiles by which people had been able to get over the wall, on the spurious grounds that the existence of gates and the presence of keepers rendered the stiles redundant. But the instructions to the keepers were that they should admit *'respectable persons'* in the daytime, and such carriages as had tickets (which were readily obtained). Common people, of course, would not be classed as 'respectable', nor would they have the luxury of a carriage. The building of Ham Gate Lodge in 1742, for example, was part of this process. Robert Walpole junior, as Ranger, continued these practices after his father's death in 1745.

Princess Amelia

In 1751 Princess Amelia (1711-1786), second daughter of George II, became Ranger on the death of Lord Orford. (She is not to be confused with the youngest daughter, and fifteenth child, of George III, another Amelia.)

Building on the successive restrictions instituted by her predecessor, Amelia simply closed the gates to everyone, with the exception of carriages whose owners were in possession of a ticket. Amelia essentially issued tickets only to her friends. When Lord Brooke, who lived at Petersham, requested a ticket the riposte was that she had denied one to the Lord Chancellor, so she was hardly going to issue one to him.

On Ascension Day 1751 the traditional 'Beating of the Parish Bounds' ceremony, led by the Vicar of Richmond parish church, took place. Ascension Day fell that year on 16 May – little more than six weeks after Amelia had taken office. In contrast to the practice in previous years, the party was not granted permission to enter the Park, but it appears that access was eventually obtained, albeit with difficulty. (See illustration opposite). Part of the wall is said to have been knocked down (but it is more likely that they just found a part of the wall which had already crumbled; a report in 1754 by the Deputy Ranger noted the very poor state of the wall, the Park roads and the drainage).

Efforts to re-establish access

The closure of the Park caused much inconvenience and resentment. Some political and legal opposition was mounted, none of it successful. A number of petitions, press notices and pamphlets met with no success. The 28 July 1752 edition of the London newspaper The Post Boy, for instance, contained a petition to the Princess from the proprietors of estates in the parishes adjoining the Park.

Resort to law was also made. A trial took place in 1754 arising from an incident in which a group of gentlemen had been refused admission to the Park. After hearing no fewer than 64 witnesses, including Lord Palmerston who gave evidence on behalf of the Princess, the court dismissed the claim.

John Lewis

Lewis (1713-1792) was a Richmond brewer. There is no record of his having attended the 1754 trial, but he would have been keenly aware of it. He would also have been aware that at nearby Bushy Park a local shoemaker, Timothy Bennet, had in the same year succeeded in persuading the Earl of Halifax to restore routes through that park which he had earlier blocked. In 1755 Lewis took a friend with him, probably a man named Shepheard, to Sheen Gate and waited until a carriage approached. The carriage, whose driver produced a ticket to the

Above: John Lewis

gatekeeper, Martha Gray, was allowed to enter the Park. Lewis then attempted to walk through the gate before it could be closed. According to a contemporary account, the following exchange occurred:

Gray: Where is your ticket?
Lewis: What occasion for a ticket? Anyone may pass through here.
Gray: No - not without a ticket.
Lewis: Yes, they may; and I will.
Gray: You shan't.
Lewis: I will.

Lewis then allowed the gate to be shut against him. On the basis of this forcible denial of access by the gatekeeper, Lewis obtained an indictment against her, although the true defendant, of course, was Princess Amelia.

The case initially came up for hearing at the Summer Assizes in August 1757. But no sooner had it opened than the defence produced in court a pamphlet which attacked Amelia and asserted the public rights of access to the Park. A 'Tract in the National Interest' had been published anonymously, stating that *The right of the people to a free passage through Richmond Park was a privilege they always enjoyed until the late Sir Robert Walpole audaciously divested them of it*.

The judge halted the trial and ordered those concerned with writing, publishing and distributing the pamphlet to be found. In his view, the pamphlet was a libel, and its distribution was a contempt of court. Lewis and Shepheard, who were in court, were accused of being involved. Lewis swore an affidavit in which he denied being concerned in *'printing or publishing the Pamphlett'*. He also denied *'dispersing any Copys'* of it. But he pointedly did not make any reference to the authorship of the pamphlet.

In spite of the suspicion that Lewis had been concerned with the pamphlets, on 13 February 1758 the court ordered that Lewis' case against Martha Gray should be resumed at the next Assizes. Just three weeks after it became known that the trial would at last take place, we find a record of what looks suspiciously like an attempt by Amelia to bribe the jury: minutes dated 5 March 1758 of the Mortlake Vestry record a gift of £50 for the purchase of a fire engine: *'....Richard Knollys Esq reported to the Gentlemen present that Her Royal Highness the Princess Amelia had given Fifty pounds to be laid out in the Purchase of an Engine for the Use of the said Parish, which has been accordingly done....'*

The case against Martha Gray eventually resumed at the Surrey Assizes, sitting at Kingston, on 3 April 1758. It appears that Amelia's gift to the citizens from whom the jury would be selected had had some effect; many refused to attend because, according to a contemporary commentator, they were reluctant to try a case against the Princess. The absentees were promptly fined £20 apiece – a huge penalty.

Lewis shrewdly confined his claim to pedestrian rights of access, and judgment was given for Lewis that day. He was asked by the court whether he wished to have a gate made in the wall or a step-ladder to go over it. He considered that a door, which would have to be kept closed when not in use, so as to prevent the escape of deer, would give the impression that access was not freely available; and he also feared that, in time, a door might have a bolt fixed to it. So he opted for the erection of ladder stiles.

On 12 May 1758 ladder stiles and gates were affixed to Sheen Gate and Ham Gate. They were opened to the public on 16 May when a *'vast concourse of people from all the neighbouring villages climbed over the ladder stiles into the Park'*. This occurred, by coincidence, exactly seven years to the day after the Ascension Day incident in 1751.

Below and top inset detail: Richmond Gate with its ladder stile (to the right) c. 1740

But Amelia had not finished yet. Some time later, Lewis went to court and complained that *'they have left such a space between the steps of the ladder that children and old men are unable to get up it'*. This account continues with the judge replying: *'I have observed it myself; and I desire, Mr Lewis, that you would see it so constructed that not only children and old men, but old women too, may be able to get up'.*

The determination of John Lewis remains a landmark in the Park's history, and worthy of being celebrated. On 16 May 2008, 250 years to the day after the new ladder stiles had been brought into use as a result of Lewis' victory, the Friends of Richmond Park erected a plaque in memory of Lewis which can be seen at Sheen Gate, the site of his confrontation with Martha Gray.

The Park after Lewis

Lewis' achievement in reclaiming for the public the right to cross the Park was indeed great, and is sometimes represented as the establishment of the rights we enjoy now. But it must be remembered that what Lewis' action was about was no more than the confirmation of pre-existing rights of way. The 'right to roam' did not come about for another century at least. Public access continued to be restricted during the first half of the 19th century: carriages were admitted only with a 'card of admission', and though pedestrians could enter freely, they were largely confined to the roads and the defined footpaths. From the 1851 Crown Lands Act onwards, the restrictions were gradually abandoned, and in 1872 the Royal Parks and Gardens Regulation Act confirmed the full right of public access to the Park.

Below: Pen Ponds c 1765 by Richard Wilson (1713 – 1782)
Opposite page top inset: 18th century cedars in 'Petersham Park'

Park Rangers

Although many monarchs from Charles I onwards took a close personal interest in the Park, its day-to-day management was undertaken by an official, originally known as the Keeper; the term Ranger was also used in the 1660s and again in the 1720s, and was the only title used after 1740. In June 1637, Charles I appointed the Earl of Portland to the position for life with a stipend of 12d. per day. Deputies in practice did most of the work, so the post was a coveted sinecure. For 12 years or so King George III kept the Rangership to himself. It was an office which clearly had some value. In 1727 the Earl of Rochester surrendered the Rangership to George II and was paid £5,000 compensation for loss of office. When Princess Amelia surrendered the office to George III (her nephew) in 1761 she was granted an annuity of £1,200. The office also appears to have brought with it certain proprietary rights: in July 1735 a complaint was made to the magistrates that a labourer called Ralph Cheshire had been seen to *'knock down one of the turkeys in His Majesty's park called New Park ... the property of Lord Walpole, Ranger...'* The fate of the poacher is not known.

In 1904, King Edward VII assumed the Rangership and gave the management of the Park to the Commissioners of Works; he instructed them that all parts of the Park should be *'more accessible to the public than hitherto'*. The Commissioners of Works became the Ministry of Works in 1945, and subsequently responsibility for all the Royal Parks passed to the Department of the Environment. The Park is part of The Royal Parks, an executive agency of the Department for Culture, Media and Sport.

Petersham Park

Petersham Park is the westernmost area of the Park. A mansion had existed here prior to the enclosure of Richmond Park, and the 1637 map shows a 'Petersham Manor House' in the area where Petersham Gate now is. That manor house became the Petersham Lodge of the Park. In 1686, King James II granted the house and 12 acres (5 ha) to the Earl of Rochester; a further 38 acres (15 ha) on the hillside were later added. Rochester demolished the mansion and built a new one; at the same time he created a large formal garden which was quite unlike anything else in the Park.

The house was destroyed by fire in 1721 and a later owner then built yet another mansion in the 1730s to the design of Lord Burlington, a great Palladian exponent of his day. The previous formal gardens were replaced with a more natural parkland. 'Petersham Park' remained formally separated from the rest of the Park until 1833, when the Crown bought it back for £14,500, and reintegrated it into the main Park. The 1730s mansion was demolished in 1835. It is this history which gives Petersham Park a noticeably different character from the rest of the Park, and some cedars from the 18th century parkland-style landscaping can still be seen.

Lady Russell had established a school in Petersham in 1849, and this was then relocated to a new building just inside Petersham Gate two years later. It was destroyed by enemy action in 1943.

Above: The Duke of Kent reviewing Phantom Squad motorcyclists 1941
Left: Ploughing the plateau north of Bog (now Holly) Lodge in 1940s
Below: Bomb sterilising pit, used for bleeding explosives from unexploded enemy bombs in WW2

Opposite page:
Bottom: Phantom Squad training in 1941
Top inset: Kingston Gate camp steps

The Park in Wartime

Like the rest of the country, the Park had to respond to the challenges of the two world wars. Food production was a priority: in the First World War, for instance, allotments were created inside Richmond Gate, and 100 acres (40ha) or so near Sheen Gate were ploughed up for oats and potatoes.

Military uses were highly visible. The area to the east of Beverley Brook (now a golf course, but then known as the Paddocks) was the site of a large camp for various volunteer brigades, and the Royal Flying Corps had a base near Killcat Corner. Between Bishop's Pond and Conduit Wood a large South African Military hospital was built in 1916 to treat wounded troops brought over from France and Belgium. Despite sophisticated treatment methods, some injured troops did not survive, and upwards of 30 graves of South African soldiers can be found in the military section of Richmond Cemetery (which can be reached by a path just outside Bog Gate).

The Second World War brought about even bigger changes. Military training was conducted in the Park, and large areas were again ploughed up for crops. The old army camp on the Paddocks had been displaced by the golf club, and a large new camp was established in 1938 to the south and east of Thatched House Lodge, to house recruits for the East Surrey Regiment. During the war the camp was a military convalescent depot for 2,500 soldiers. After the war, it served as an athletics village for the 1948 London Olympic Games, and housed the Royal Corps of Signals and repatriated service families from Suez in 1956. It was eventually demolished in 1965. Anti-aircraft gun emplacements were set up in a number of locations, and, as a further defensive measure, Pen Ponds were drained and camouflaged so as to deny bomber crews the sight of a recognisable landmark. A facility for disabling unexploded bombs operated between Isabella Plantation and Ham Cross.

Pembroke Lodge was the base of the GHQ Liaison Regiment known as "Phantom" Squad, a secret regiment set up to train armoured car personnel and motorcycle riders to patrol the battlefront in Europe and relay intelligence back. Training was done in the Park.

Buildings

By Michael Davison, Friends of Richmond Park Volunteer

Richmond Park contains a wealth of historic buildings, from hunting lodges which have been extended into grand houses, to humbler keepers' cottages and a functional conduit and well. The oldest dates from 1500, with many more from the 17th to the 19th centuries. Five of these buildings are listed by English Heritage as being of special architectural or historic interest.

Pembroke Lodge

A molecatcher, a prime minister, two earls, five countesses, a child who was to become a renowned philosopher and a group of wartime special agents: all have been residents of Pembroke Lodge at some time in its long history. Alterations and extensions made by successive occupants over the years have created the stately, white-walled Georgian mansion with its columned porch that stands on the brow of a hill near the Park's western edge.

The house began in the early 18th century as a one-room cottage built for the Park's molecatcher. In 1702 William III had died after a fall from his horse when it stumbled on a molehill at Hampton Court. His successors who hunted in Richmond Park took no chances and employed a royal molecatcher. He did a good job: to this day there are no moles in the Park.

The cottage was enlarged and, as Hill Lodge, became the home of a gamekeeper, John Trage. He let rooms to Elizabeth, Countess of Pembroke, who fell in love with the Lodge and begged George III to grant it to her. One of the great beauties of the day, she got her way. The Countess then began a long process of enlargements to the property in the 1780s and 90s, by leading architects of the day Sir John Soane and Henry Holland. The entire Georgian wing, facing today's visitors as they pass between the handsome new entrance pillars, dates from this time.

After the Countess of Pembroke died in 1831, William IV granted the Lodge, which by then bore the Countess' name, to his son-in-law the Earl of Erroll, who had married Elizabeth FitzClarence, one of the King's illegitimate daughters. Erroll completed work on the north wing. After the Earl's death in 1846, the Lodge returned to the Pembroke family, being occupied for a short period by the Countess of Dunmore, the granddaughter of the Countess of Pembroke and, like her, a Lady of the Bedchamber to the Queen.

Another visitor who, like the Countess of Pembroke, fell in love with the Lodge, was Lord John Russell. A railed-in oak tree at the upper end of the car park marks the spot where in 1845, a year before becoming Queen Victoria's Prime Minister, Russell and his wife sat while visiting Richmond in search of a country home. Sitting on a bench under this oak they looked into the grounds of Pembroke Lodge and, as Lady Russell recalled, *'We said to one another that would be the place for us!'*

In 1847 Queen Victoria granted the Russells the Lodge, and for 30 years it became a place both of Cabinet business and of high society functions, whose visitors included the Queen and Prince Albert, Lord Palmerston, William Gladstone, Benjamin Disraeli, Charles Dickens, Lord Tennyson and Lewis Carroll. Lord John Russell accepted an earldom in 1861, and died at Pembroke Lodge in 1878. A memorial to the Russells' 'supremely happy home' stands in the rose garden.

This page, clockwise from top
Lord and Lady Russell, with some of their family, in Pembroke Lodge gardens 1865
Terrace wedding function
Views from Pembroke Lodge

Bertrand Russell, philosopher and mathematician, spent his early years at Pembroke Lodge when, at the age of four, he was taken in by the Russells, his grandparents, after the death of his own parents. He wrote of his affection for the house, with its *'wide horizons and unimpeded view of the sunset'.*

From 1903 yet another countess, Georgina Countess of Dudley, occupied the Lodge and made further alterations, including the decorative friezes and mahogany doors much admired by today's café visitors, as did its next occupant, industrialist John Scott Oliver.

The Second World War brought a new phase in Pembroke Lodge's history, when it was requisitioned for military use by the GHQ Liaison Regiment, known as 'Phantom'. This was a secret unit set up to train armoured car personnel and motorcycle riders equipped with radios to patrol the battlefront in Europe and relay intelligence to the commanders of Allied units – a role described by Field Marshal Montgomery as 'indispensable'. Among the unit's officers was the film actor David Niven, who described his time at Pembroke Lodge as being *'wonderful days which I would not have missed for anything'.*

The post-war years brought a sad episode in the Lodge's history, as the building gradually crumbled with nothing but a small tea-room in public use. Years of uncertainty over its future were finally ended when in 1996 Daniel Hearsum, a chartered surveyor, took a long lease on the Lodge. Its north wing was by then a derelict shell, and Hearsum embarked on seven years of spectacular refurbishment to restore the mansion to the grace of its 19th century heyday.

The restoration of the property has also given today's Park visitors a spacious new cafeteria, first-floor function rooms containing displays of Russell family and Phantom memorabilia collected by Daniel Hearsum, and a glazed Georgian-style pavilion, the Belvedere, a popular venue for weddings and other ceremonies. A broad terrace looks across Petersham to the Thames.

Top inset: Police station at Holly Lodge
Below: Holly Lodge: Park offices in a country cottage

Holly Lodge

There is a homely simplicity about the appearance of Holly Lodge which sets it apart from other, grander mansions in the Park. The visitor passes through an immaculately maintained cottage-style garden, then enters the house through a graceful porch of white-painted lattice work.

Holly Lodge is the Park's administrative centre, housing the offices of the Park Superintendent and his team, and it is also the headquarters of the Park's police. An information desk is open to the public on weekdays. At the rear are stables for the Park's resident Shire horses, a blacksmith's forge, a sawmill, and a carpenter's workshop where wood from the Park is turned into posts, palings, benches and 'cages' for young trees. Other outbuildings include the first timber-framed building constructed in the Park for 300 years, using entirely traditional tools and joinery. In this are stored the implements used by the Shire horses.

In addition the Lodge has an important educational function. The Holly Lodge Centre, opened in 1994, is a charitable organisation whose volunteers provide a range of activities designed to teach groups of people, especially those with special needs, about the Park, its wildlife and the natural environment. The Centre is wheechair-accessible, with a nature trail, a pond for 'dipping' to discover water life, and art and craft sessions. A reconstructed Victorian kitchen and schoolroom, and a kitchen garden, help visitors learn what life was like in Victorian times. In 2010 the Centre added a reconstructed chemist's shop, its contents coming from a former pharmacy in East Sheen where they had been preserved in their original condition.

Starting just beyond the western gate of Holly Lodge there stretches a line of some of the Park's most ancient oak trees, stout and gnarled. These marked the boundary of Hill Farm, which included the site of the present lodge at the time of the Park's enclosure. The farm was replaced in 1735 by a new building for the Head Keeper, taking the name of Cooper's Lodge, then Lucas's Lodge, after two successive incumbents.

For more than a century from 1795 three generations of the Sawyer family occupied the Lodge as Head Keepers. During their time the building became known as Bog Lodge, after marshy ground nearby which was drained in the 19th century. In the 1990s the Lodge adopted its more sympathetic present name.

Open Days at Holly Lodge give visitors the chance to watch traditional crafts such as charcoal burning, fence making, wood carving and hedge laying, and to learn about the Park's deer and trees. There are displays by organisations concerned with the Park and its wildlife, including the Friends of Richmond Park.

White Lodge

The magnificent classical building in white Portland stone, whose high position makes it a landmark from many points in the Park, was the creation of a king – and has been associated over the years with a veritable roll-call of royal residents.

George I was the monarch who in 1726 found the need to build a hunting lodge and banqueting house to use during his visits to Richmond for 'the diversion of hunting in the Park'. His two architects, Roger Morris and Henry, Lord Herbert, built in the currently fashionable Palladian revival style which they had already adopted for Marble Hill in Twickenham. In White Lodge they created a mansion that nearly three centuries later is protected as the Park's only Grade I listed building.

George I died in 1727 before the building was completed, so his son was the first to make full use of it, often together with his hunting Prime Minister, Sir Robert Walpole. It was George II's wife, Caroline, who had the Queen's Ride cut through the existing woodland to create a grand avenue along which to journey between her hunting lodge and Richmond Lodge, a royal home in the Old Deer Park. She entered and left Richmond Park by a specially built Queen's Gate, now Bog Gate. Caroline died only a year after the ride was completed.

The Lodge has not always had its present name. Originally called Stone Lodge, it later became New Lodge to distinguish it from an earlier mansion which once stood about a quarter of a mile to the south, near the present-day Pen Ponds car park. By 1760 the name White Lodge had come into use. Shortly before then the building had been augmented by two pavilions, linked to the main building at first by underground tunnels, but later by two semi-circular galleries.

Opposite page: Holly Lodge stables and Shire horse
This page: top inset: The Crest of the Ballet School at White Lodge
Below: White Lodge: from Royal Hunting Lodge to Royal Ballet School

An important new period for White Lodge commenced in 1801 when George III granted the house as a 'grace and favour' residence to his Prime Minister Henry Addington, later Lord Sidmouth. Appointed Deputy Ranger in 1813 and holding the post until his death in 1844, Sidmouth was a man with a passion for trees, whose carefully planned woodland plantations and trees round the wall are largely responsible for the look of the Park we know today.

Sidmouth enlarged White Lodge and played host there to many of the great and good of the time, just as Lord John Russell was later to do at Pembroke Lodge. Sidmouth's guests included George III, William Pitt the Younger, and the writers Richard Sheridan and Sir Walter Scott. The Lodge's Nelson Room commemorates a meeting in September 1805 at which Nelson is said to have traced out, with a finger dipped in wine on a table, the battle tactics which were to lead to his great victory the following month at Trafalgar.

After Sidmouth's death the Lodge passed back into royal hands. Victoria and Albert stayed there, and in 1869 it was presented to the Duke and Duchess of Teck. They lived at the Lodge for almost 30 years, and their daughter Queen Mary, consort to George V, spent her childhood there.

In 1894 the Lodge was the birth-place of George V and Mary's eldest son who briefly became Edward VIII in 1936, before abdicating. From 1923 the Duke and Duchess of York, later George VI and Queen Elizabeth, spent the early years of their married life at the Lodge.

In 1954 White Lodge found an entirely new role when Sadler's Wells Ballet School took a lease on the building. Today it remains the home of what is now the Royal Ballet Lower School. The school's motto 'Strength and Grace' appears at the handsome new entrance gates which were part of a major refurbishment and extension of the Lodge to equip the school for the needs of the 21st century.

The White Lodge Museum and Ballet Resource Centre occupies a crescent wing of the Lodge and is open to the public on certain days. There are occasional open days when visitors can tour the remainder of the building. The museum shows the history of classical ballet and the history of White Lodge on parallel timelines.

Below left: Sculpture of ballet dancers
Below right: North wing of White Lodge
Opposite page: Thatched House Lodge, home to a Princess
Top inset: Gate detail

Thatched House Lodge

'Thatched? But it's not thatched!' protest newcomers on confronting the slate-roofed 18th-century mansion on rising ground near Kingston Gate. In fact the Lodge takes its name not from the building itself, but from a thatched summer house in the four-acre (1.5 ha) grounds, visible through the trees in winter.

The Lodge itself dates from 1673, when it became 'a convenient abiding place' for two employees of the Keeper of the Park, the Duke of Lauderdale. Later it became known as Aldridge's Lodge after Charles Aldridge, another Keeper.

The next step in the piecemeal development of the Lodge came with the appointment of Sir Robert Walpole as Britain's first prime minister in 1721. Walpole was a keen huntsman and spent £14,000 (more than £1 million today) improving the Lodge and other buildings in the Park. It was Walpole who added the summer house with its thatched roof and octagonal hall, perhaps as a secluded place to entertain Molly Skerrett, his mistress, who later became his second wife; it may also have been used by George II when he came hunting with his Prime Minister. By 1771 the name of Thatched House Lodge came to be used for the entire property.

The front of the building was remodelled in the 1790s by John Soane, the architect who also gave Pembroke Lodge its present appearance, and a new west wing was added in the 1880s. It is this building that in 1963 became the home of Princess Alexandra and Sir Angus Ogilvy after their marriage. They took it on commercial terms on a long lease, its former 'grace and favour' status having ended in 1927. After Angus Ogilvy's death in 2004, the Lodge remained Princess Alexandra's private residence and is not open to the public.

General Sir William Medows, one of many distinguished residents of Thatched House Lodge over the years, commissioned painted decorations in neo-classical style for the summer house in the 1770s. Mural designs formed the background to a series of oil paintings of classical scenes long attributed to Angelica Kaufmann, but later identified as being the work of her husband, Antonio Zucchi. The paintings were removed in 1978, and have since passed into private hands.

White Ash Lodge

Outside the fence surrounding White Ash Lodge, patches of stone and brick under the trees are the remains of extensive outbuildings which once adjoined the surviving brick-built farmhouse. The Lodge is one of the Park's earliest buildings. It was first recorded in 1754, but probably built in the 1730s or 1740s at about the same time as Holly Lodge, which has a similar bow window in its west wall.

White Ash Lodge was the home of a succession of Park deputy keepers. Its outbuildings included pigsties and chicken houses, and a venison house where deer carcases were hung before being prepared for the table. Near the Lodge was a pen in which fallow deer were fed during winter.

An ancient but flourishing Mulberry tree stands in the garden of the house, which is privately occupied.

Oak Lodge

The collection of buildings at the southern end of Sidmouth Wood, with two conspicuous Monkey-Puzzle trees among the oaks which give the Lodge its name, began life around 1852 as a home for the park bailiff, responsible for repairs and maintenance in the Park. It serves a similar function today, as the base of operations for the hard-working teams who tend the Park's open spaces, woodlands, paths and gardens.

The main building is in brick, with a slate roof. The outbuildings provide facilities for the litter clearers and the estate maintenance team. They flank a courtyard where horticultural and stable waste is composted for use in tree planting and as garden mulch. There is also an area for the Park's litter skips and recycling bins. A charcoal burner makes charcoal and processes firewood.

White Conduit and Well House

Two small buildings unnoticed by many visitors bear witness to the use once made of springs on the high land of Richmond Park as a source of fresh water for settlements in Richmond and Petersham below.

The earliest of these is the White Conduit, a long low structure half-hidden in the woods not far from Richmond Gate. Beneath a curved roof are the remains of a cistern re-built around 1500, and of an adjacent, somewhat later one, to collect water from nearby springs and channel it to the palace just re-built by Henry VII at Richmond. There remain traces of the Tudor brickwork.

The brick was probably once plastered, giving the building its formal name. The concrete casing added in Victorian times has led locals to refer to it less reverently as the 'bomb shelter' or the 'Nissen hut'. In the 20th century the Conduit supplied water to the South African Military Hospital near Richmond Gate.

Around 1800, springs in the Park were tapped again. Tucked into the slope below the gardens of Pembroke Lodge is an igloo-like brick building that is often mistaken for an ice-house. It is in fact a well house storing water from a spring under the hill nearby.

The water from this well house was channelled downhill to Petersham Lodge, a mansion built at the foot of the slope in the 18th century. This building was the last in a succession of lodges at the heart of an estate which for nearly two centuries formed a separate enclave within Richmond Park. After the demolition of the last lodge in 1835, the water may have been diverted to supply Russell School, established near Petersham Gate in 1851 by the Russell family of Pembroke Lodge, but destroyed in the Second World War.

Water from the well still emerges from a tunnel about 50 metres (160ft) down the slope and trickles down the hillside.

Opposite page:
Bottom: Stable at White Ash Lodge

This page:
Below: Well House
Bottom: White Conduit
Top inset: Wooden seat and bicycle rack at White Lodge

The Wall near Ham Gate
Opposite page, top inset: The freebord
outside Bishop's Gate

The Wall, Gates and Other Structures
By Michael Davison

In addition to its historic residences, Richmond Park embraces a variety of other man-made structures – from the entrance gates and their lodges (two of them Grade II listed) to the massive eight-mile wall which encloses the Park. A prominent prehistoric mound offers views stretching far beyond the Park's boundary.

The Wall

The great wall round Richmond Park is such a familiar sight that it is easy to forget what a mammoth building project it was for its time – or indeed for any time. To enclose his new hunting park, Charles I required nothing less than a brick wall eight miles (13km) long and 9ft (2.7m) high. Added to the scale of the task, the builder who gained the contract, Edward Manning, faced a further challenge. Even in an age used to the autocratic ways of monarchs, local people did not take kindly to the loss of their lands, with the result that Manning found it hard to recruit local labour for the task. A bit of royal press ganging, however, did the trick; 'mayors and kings' officers' were instructed to assist Manning in 'taking up the required bricklayers, labourers, carts and carriages'.

In 1635 Manning's men went to work. At that time building in brick was not as commonplace as it is today, for bricks were a relatively recent innovation which only the wealthy could afford. The bricks for the Park wall had to be specially made on site from local London clay, and the sky over Richmond was smoky from the fires that heated the kilns. It has been estimated that some five million bricks were made and laid.

The job was finished in 1637, in less than three years, and Manning was paid his promised £2,500 – as it worked out, a pound per acre enclosed. He did not, in truth, do a terribly good job, for the wall soon started crumbling and extensive repairs were needed. Over the centuries keeping the wall intact has proved an endless task, which continues to this day, in order to maintain what is officially classified by English Heritage as a Grade II listed structure. The task of repairing the outer surface of the wall is aided by the historic 'freebord', a strip of land 16ft 6in (5m) wide retained round the perimeter of the Park when the Wall was built, except where it adjoined existing Crown land. The freebord is not always visible today, but a stretch of it can be clearly seen outside Bishop's Gate.

Although the wall is often described as totally enclosing the Park except at the gates, there are in fact several gaps where, in the 18th and 19th centuries, influential landowners of properties bordering the Park secured an uninterrupted view or an extension to their lands. These include short sections at Kingston Hill Place on Broomfield Hill, at Ancaster House beside Richmond Gate, and at Petersham Gate, with a longer gap alongside Sudbrook Park. Outside Roehampton Gate the wall is replaced by railings for half a mile, but a further section of the wall survives out of sight beyond the golf course.

The age of different sections of the wall can be estimated by the way the bricks are laid. The original builders used what is called 'English bond'. In this method layers, or courses, of bricks laid lengthways (called 'stretchers') alternate with courses laid with the narrow end of the brick outward (called 'headers'). Later builders repairing the wall switched to the more decorative 'Flemish bond' in which each course consists of alternate stretchers and headers.

The Gates

When Charles I enclosed Richmond Park in 1637 he allowed local people access through six gates. These remain major entry points to the Park, although the gates themselves have been replaced over the years and they have been supplemented by five additional public entrances. Lodges that were built to accommodate gatekeepers still stand, some in altered form, but their incumbents who once controlled entry and later nodded a cheery greeting to visitors have been succeeded by private occupants.

The Six Early Gates

Richmond Gate

Still framing the grandest entry to the Park, the gates of 1798 bear the cyphers of GR for George III and CR for his queen, Charlotte. Together with the adjoining lodge, with its stuccoed brick walls and slate roof, they were designed by John Soane, architect of the Bank of England, who worked also on Pembroke Lodge. The gates were widened in the early 20th century to make room for three carriageways.

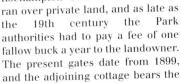

East Sheen Gate

History was made at East Sheen Gate in 1755 when John Lewis, a Richmond brewer, was barred from entering the Park at a time when Princess Amelia, Park Ranger, denied access to all but her chosen friends. He took the offending gatekeeper to court and by winning his case secured the right of public access to Richmond Park which all now enjoy. A plaque set on the gatepost in 2008 by the Friends of Richmond Park commemorates the 250th anniversary of the success of Lewis' court action.

Roehampton Gate

The approach to Roehampton Gate ran over private land, and as late as the 19th century the Park authorities had to pay a fee of one fallow buck a year to the landowner. The present gates date from 1899, and the adjoining cottage bears the prominent monogram 'VRI' for Victoria Regina Imperatrix (Queen and Empress)

with the date 1900. Just outside the gate on the left, a narrow lane with the sinister nickname of Cut-throat Alley dating from its unsavoury past leads alongside Beverley Brook to Palewell Common.

Opposite page:
Top: Soane's lodge at Richmond Gate
Middle: George III Royal cypher
Bottom: Richmond Gate (with the Royal Star & Garter Home behind)

This page:
Left above: Octagonal tower house outside Sheen Gate
Left: John Lewis' plaque and mileages
Below: Roehampton Gate with Cut-throat Alley to the right
Top inset: Queen Charlotte's cypher

Robin Hood Gate

Known until 1750 as Wimbledon Gate, Robin Hood Gate was renamed after an inn built nearby at the height of the stagecoach era. The Robin Hood Inn was part of Robin Hood Farm, named after May Games featuring 'Robin Hood' and his associates, which are said to have been held in this area in medieval times. The present gates bear the monogram of Edward VII and the date of 1907.

Ladderstile Gate

Ladderstiles were installed beside the six gates left by Charles I so that people could enter the Park even when the gates were locked. A ladderstile at what was once known as Coombe Gate was removed during the 1740s but replaced after John Lewis secured public access in 1758. This was the last ladderstile to be replaced by a pedestrian gate, in 1884, and its present name commemorates this historic means of access. A new gate was added in 1901. The adjoining lodge dates from the 1780s.

Ham Gate

Decorative lantern lights, still lit by gas, adorn the columns at either side of the wrought-iron gates, which were installed in 1921 when the entrance was widened. The adjoining lodge was built in 1742 and is said to be the only Park lodge surviving in its original state. Beside the lodge still stands a small hut with black weather-boarded walls, once used as a shelter by Park police.

Above top: Robin Hood Gate
Above: Detail of the gates which were built in 1907
Right above: Ladderstile Gate and Lodge
Right: Old post box and mileage plaque at Ham Gate, and decorative gas lantern

The Five Later Gates

Bishop's Gate

Two assistant Park keepers, father and son, gave their name to this gate and the adjoining lodge. In the 19th century the gate was used to bring cattle into the Park for grazing. Just outside the gate, walkers briefly follow a path parallel to the wall. This is a section of the historic 'freebord', described in the section on the Wall.

Cambrian Gate

During the First World War a South African Military Hospital covered 12 acres (5ha) of land between Richmond Gate and Conduit Wood. To allow quick access to ambulances bringing the wounded from Richmond Station, a new gate was cut into the wall at the top of Cambrian Road, and when the hospital was demolished in 1925 the gate became a public entrance.

Below right: Bishop's Gate
Below left: The old Park police hut at Ham Gate
Bottom: Cambrian Gate
Top inset: Robin Hood Gate detail

Petersham Gate

Where Petersham Gate now stands was once the grand entrance to Petersham Park, for more than 150 years a separate estate within Richmond Park and the site of no fewer than three successive lodges, all now lost. The cedar trees visible from the gate are survivors from ornamental plantings on the estate. Petersham Park was reincorporated into Richmond Park in 1833. A school built by Lord and Lady Russell just inside the gate in 1851 was destroyed by a bomb in 1943.

Bog Gate

Originally this was Queen's Gate. It was made in 1736 as a private entrance by which Queen Caroline, consort of George II, could enter and leave the Park on her journeys between White Lodge and Richmond Lodge in the Old Deer Park. The marshland which earned the gate its later name was drained in the 19th century. The gate leads today onto East Sheen Common, a continuation of Richmond Park's green spaces.

Kingston Gate

Today's much-used principal access into Richmond Park from Kingston did not exist until a century after Charles I's enclosure, being first shown on a map of 1754. In 1861 Queen Victoria opened a new pair of iron gates, and for a while the entrance was locally called Queen's Gate. The present gates date from the 1950s. The lodge, first shown on a 1911 map, replaced an earlier building on the opposite side of the road.

Above: Bog Gate from Sheen Common
Top right: Petersham Gate
Middle: Ian Dury's bench
Bottom: A 10 mile 'corridor' leads the eye from King Henry's Mound to St Paul's Cathedral

Opposite page:
Bottom: Seat with a view at Poet's Corner near King Henry's Mound
Top inset: Plaque marking distance to St Paul's

King Henry VIII's Mound

A man-made creation older than any building of brick or stone in the Park is the prominent earth mound rising at the northern end of the grounds of Pembroke Lodge.

It is known as King Henry VIII's Mound, though it predates Henry by more than 2,000 years, being a 'barrow' or burial mound dating from Bronze Age times. Opened in 1835, the mound was found to contain 'a considerable deposit of ashes', confirming that it once protected the remains of early farmers who settled in the area before 900 BC.

The name of Henry VIII became attached to the mound as early as 1754 through a legend that Henry stood there on 19 May 1536, awaiting a signal from the Tower of London to indicate that his Queen, Anne Boleyn, had been executed. In fact the King is known to have been in Wiltshire at the time, so unfortunately the legend is not true. A map made before the Park's enclosure marked the mound more simply as 'The King's Standinge', suggesting that monarchs may have used it as a viewpoint from which to watch hunting or falconry in the Park.

From the top of the Mound, the highest point in the Park at 57m (187ft), there are stunning views westward across Petersham and the Thames towards Windsor Castle, and north-east to St Paul's Cathedral, 10 miles (16km) away. The view of St Paul's was created soon after the Cathedral was completed in 1710 by planting an avenue of trees from the Mound leading the eye towards it. This vista, clear of tall buildings, was maintained over the years, but was obliterated by unchecked tree growth during the Second World War. The view was re-created in 1976, and since then the chestnut trees along the line of sight have been kept carefully cut back.

In the 1970s this view came under threat because of plans to develop Liverpool Street Station with the erection of a high-rise building. A local campaign stopped the building and in 1992 the vista became a protected view. The width of the protected view was halved in 2007 by the Mayor of London, Ken Livingstone, to allow more high-rise office blocks. In 2009, Boris Johnson, his successor, promised to reinstate the wider view, but not before approving a development at Victoria Station, which will obscure its lower right-hand corner.

Between the Mound and the north gate of Pembroke Lodge Gardens is Poet's Corner, where a rustic panel pays tribute to James Thomson (1700 - 1748). Just outside the gate is an ironwork seat bearing lines from Thomson's poem

"The Seasons". The seat is a memorial to Ramon Osner, a director of the Kingston Riding Centre, who rode in the Park for almost 20 years until his death in 1990. Also near the Mound is a solar powered musical bench with sockets for earphones to listen to songs by rock musician Ian Dury (1942 - 2000) who enjoyed walking in the Park.

Shire horses at work in the Park
Top inset: Entrance to the offices at Holly Lodge

Management of Richmond Park

By Simon Richards, Park Superintendent.

Richmond Park is one of eight parks managed by The Royal Parks (TRP) on behalf of The Queen, who owns the parks in right of the Crown. It is operated day to day by an internal management team of eight people, and around 140 full-time outside contractors, including landscape and building maintenance teams, gardeners, arboriculturists, litter pickers, catering and golf course staff.

Richmond Park was enclosed by Charles I and continues to be owned by the Crown. From 1637 to 1904, it was also managed by a Ranger (called a Keeper in the early days) who was appointed by the King or Queen. The Ranger was typically a sinecure for a member of the royal circle and the real work was done by the Deputies. In 1904, King Edward VII gave the management to the government, where it remains in the shape of The Royal Parks (TRP).

TRP is part of the Department for Culture, Media and Sport (DCMS), which also has responsibility for museums, the Sports and Arts Councils and the BBC, although as I write in summer 2010, the new coalition government has announced plans to transfer responsibility for the Royal Parks to the Mayor of London.

Being managed by national government reflects the fact that the Royal Parks are a national resource and therefore are funded by central rather than local government. Thus the residents of Berwick-upon-Tweed pay the same proportion of their income for the upkeep of Richmond Park as the residents of East Sheen. National as well as local objectives are important, which is particularly relevant where, say, the condition of our acid grassland is measured against a national standard and our statutory duty to meet these standards may perhaps conflict with a local desire for unfettered access.

Each of the eight Royal Parks is managed directly by a Park Manager (Park Superintendent as we are still known to many). We individually report to the Director of Parks within TRP. Our management board, which includes non-executive members from outside government, reports to the Secretary of State who is ultimately accountable for our performance to Parliament. An annual report is published each year and is scrutinised by the cross-party Public Accounts Committee.

In government terms, TRP is a miniscule organisation. It received a government grant of £19m in 2009/10, about a third of the current cost of rebuilding a motorway junction on the M25. In addition, TRP generates commercial income of £13m (from Hyde Park concerts, catering concessions etc), giving a total income and expenditure of £32m. Richmond Park accounts for about £2.5m of the £32m. TRP has had considerable success in recent years in increasing income to offset a reducing government grant. This drive to increase income to maintain and enhance services is not without its difficulties.

The purpose of The Royal Parks as defined by the Secretary of State is 'to manage the Royal Parks efficiently and effectively; balancing the responsibility to conserve and enhance these unique environments with creative policies to encourage access and to increase opportunities for enjoyment, education, entertainment and healthy recreation.'

Underlying this purpose is a set of six corporate objectives, which are framed to support the strategic priorities and wider responsibilities of DCMS. Thus, for instance, TRP will have a role to play in helping the government of the day meet national targets for reducing obesity. I do not propose to list these or any of the array of supporting documentation, strategies and policies. These are all available to scholars and insomniacs as public documents, most easily via the TRP website www.royalparks.org.uk.

However it is probably worth mentioning the Green Flag awards to those who may have noticed a rather fetching lime green flag flying in the breeze at Holly Lodge. The Green Flag Awards are a national scheme which promotes high standards across parks. Each year TRP enter all their parks into the competition and the parks are judged. Many of the TRP staff also act as judges for other sites and such competitions do much to share best practice and drive up standards.

To manage Richmond Park – the largest enclosed urban park in Europe – a total of eight people are directly employed by TRP, and are based at Holly Lodge. Apart from the Park Superintendent, or Manager, there are two Assistant Park Managers, who are responsible for all day-to-day operations; an Office Manager and two assistants, who manage our finances and public reception duties, as well as dealing with events, filming and general administrative support; and two Wildlife Officers, who are primarily responsible for managing the historic deer herds. In recent years, TRP has increased the central support it provides from Hyde Park, and a Park Services team now provides support for landscape design, events and filming, education and community engagement, ecology and arboriculture.

This relatively small management team masks the fact that Richmond Park is actually a substantial employer locally through out-sourced services. In the early 1990s many of the services which were previously operated directly such as gardening were packaged up and put out to tender to the private sector.

Some 140 people are now employed as full-time equivalents in outsourced services and it is they who keep the Park functioning day-to-day. It may go some way to explaining the liveries of the various vans that are seen circulating the Park. The key individual areas are run as follows:

The Landscape Maintenance contract is run by a firm of outside contractors, who are employed to carry out all of the traditional horticultural operations, including planting, watering and aftercare of young trees, spring and summer seasonal and herbaceous planting, maintenance of paths and ditches, sports pitch maintenance, mowing, hay cutting, bracken rolling and cutting and small landscape improvements. The staff are based at Oak Lodge, Pembroke Lodge and the Isabella Plantation. This team is also responsible for clearing litter and all the other detritus left by our millions of visitors. They also employ the staff who look after the Shire horses in the Park.

Opposite page: Feeding the deer in winter

This page:
Bottom: A hay rick for the deer near Saw Pit Wood
Below: Woods near Sheen Gate car park

Top inset: Detail of Art Nouveau gate at Isabella

Re-cycling the Park's timber for tree crates from top left clockwise:
Inspecting the tree for bats prior to work
Felling a tree for timber
Preparing a log for the sawmill
The sawmill in action
Tree crates that protect young trees for 40 years

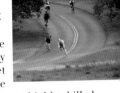

Many of the staff are the same as were originally employed directly by TRP. The fact that the operating company changes every few years (at the time of writing we are now on our fourth main contract, two of which have been subject to takeovers midway through) means that many of the gardeners are now with their sixth employer in 18 years. They certainly never run out of green T-shirts!

We spend a similar amount each year maintaining the built fabric of the park as we do the landscape. Much of this fabric, such as the boundary wall and lodges, is listed. A large firm of facilities management contractors manage this, with a small team based at the Park, backed up by specialist service providers who will, for instance, come in to carry out wall repairs. Some eight miles (13km) of roads (which are actually private roads) and car parks also need maintaining. Although over 90 per cent of the 10 million cars that use the park annually is through traffic, we get no additional support to maintain the roads.

Other service contractors carry out the toilet cleaning and gate locking, and there are highly skilled arboricultural teams who have developed a specialism for working on our ancient trees and have been able to spread this best practice to other landowners across the south of England. TRP still maintains a Nursery at Hyde Park and many of the plants that decorate the spring and summer floral displays are grown there.

The golf courses, which are managed by a specialist golf course company under a 20-year concession, employ not only green keepers, but also golf professionals and retail and catering staff. The golf courses provide TRP with a substantial annual income.

Below: Harvested timber taken to the sawmill
Top inset: Eight miles of roadway run around the Park

Catering services are perhaps the biggest employer in the Park, with Pembroke Lodge being the largest operation by far. It is also operated under a long-term concession and has been restored from a derelict shell to one of the best public catering operations in London with the busiest wedding venue in West London. Pembroke Lodge can be operating for 18 hours a day, seven days a week at peak times. Elsewhere, Roehampton café and the various mobile operations are also very busy.

Smaller concessions such as kite boarding and cycle hire, as well as licensed fitness and Nordic Walking instructors, all contribute to the diversity of services offered to the public, which complement some of the targets set for TRP.

The management centre at Holly Lodge is also the base for the Metropolitan Police unit in the Park. Until 2004, the parks were policed by the Royal Parks Constabulary (RPC). Following a review of policing, it was decided to absorb the RPC into the Metropolitan Police. At this time a substantial proportion of the Royal Parks' budget was transferred to the Home Office to fund the Metropolitan Police takeover. Regrettably at that time, the decision was made to wind up the RPC Mounted Section and now a mounted police presence is a rare event.

The Police are split into two teams: a response team with two police on duty 15 hours a day who respond to incidents, and a 'Safer Parks Team', which includes Police Community Support Officers, who are primarily responsible for the enforcement of Park Regulations and whose priorities are set by the community-based Safer Parks Panel.

It would not be possible to provide many of the facilities that we do without the support of a dedicated and growing band of volunteers. Our key partners here are The Friends of Richmond Park, The Holly Lodge Centre charity and the Richmond Park Wildlife Group. Between these three groups we now have well over 200 active volunteers.

The Friends staff the Visitor Centre, lead walks and work on conservation projects. The Holly Lodge Centre was opened in 1993 and provides a range of opportunities for those with special needs.

The Richmond Park Wildlife Group represents many stakeholders interested in protecting the Park's wildlife and regularly meets with the Park management team to discuss issues surrounding flora and fauna and to agree future programmes of work. Specialist sub-groups represent flora, birds, butterflies and invertebrates. A network of volunteer recorders actively monitor a range of species each year, which is now giving TRP a far more accurate indication of the performance of key species over time.

Other support for the Park comes in the form of The Royal Parks Foundation and the Richmond Park Charitable Trust. The former is a separate charity that fundraises on behalf of the Royal Parks and supports projects across all of the Parks, including campaigns to sponsor trees and benches as well as larger, one-off commissions. The latter is a private charity, originally formed to construct the Tamsin Trail. Since this time it has supported other Park

projects such as the new horse ride around Gibbet Wood and a variety of water conservation projects such as the construction and restoration of ponds.

I am often asked what constitutes a typical day in my role as Park Superintendent. There is really no such thing as a typical day and the idea that I spend the day roaming the Park counting the deer is regrettably rather far-fetched. The reality often seems to be a series of meetings interspersed with intense bouts of e-mailing! However there can be few jobs which offer such a wide variety of challenges and I often say that although my background was originally in horticultural management, I need to be able to communicate with architects, engineers, planners, ecologists, deer specialists, nurserymen and civil servants to name but a few. All of this in the face of a demanding role trying to resolve conflicts between the different user groups within the Park.

At this time we are lucky that the entire management team are resident in Park lodges. This gives a high level of incidental supervision of the Park, whether or not on duty, which was particularly beneficial, for example, during the heavy snowfalls of early 2010. We were able to be on duty in the early hours of the morning to co-ordinate snow clearing operations and to ensure that the children at The Royal Ballet School were able to receive fresh food and would be able to get out of the Park in emergencies. Occasions such as this would be far more difficult to manage if the team was resident miles away.

Looking to the future, there will be many continuing challenges. Of these perhaps climate change and staff skills will be particularly testing. Climate change may have the capacity to completely alter our landscape and we are already seeing our trees becoming threatened by a multiplicity of pests and diseases which are adversely affecting their health. Future tree planting strategies will have to be carefully planned with this in mind.

It is a fact that many of our operations rely on the long term skills and knowledge of an ageing workforce. This potential loss of knowledge could be critical for the future survival of the gardens at the Isabella Plantation and Pembroke Lodge. For this reason, the Royal Parks re-established an apprenticeship scheme in 2007 and each year the Park is taking on one apprentice, with the result that we now have three apprentices working in the Park on a three-year programme. Although there is no guarantee of employment in the Park at the end of the term, the skills learnt will be invaluable to these apprentices when seeking employment in the horticultural industry. It is also a fact that many apprentices go on to be leading figures in the industry and in the past several have returned to the Royal Parks in a variety of capacities.

No two days are ever the same, and, whatever happens, managing the Park is never dull. I suspect that the enjoyment most of us have for our jobs explains why turnover of staff tends to be pretty low. We may have many corporate aims and pressures, but really there is only one thing that we seek to achieve, and that is to hand the Park over to those that come after us in at least as good a condition as when we inherited it.

Commuting on a winter morning
Top inset: Signposts near Pen Ponds
car park

DOs and DONTs

By Ron Crompton, Chairman, Friends of Richmond Park.

Richmond Park is there for everyone to enjoy, whatever they are doing. But it is also a fragile ecology. Following some basic guidelines will help you 'tread lightly' and leave it in as good a state as you found it.

Richmond Park is one of the few large open spaces in London that allow people to get away from the hustle and bustle of a big city, and enjoy peace and tranquillity. It offers space for a wide range of activities, including walking, running, cycling, dog walking, flying kites and model aircraft, and horse riding. Whatever you are doing, please remember that Richmond Park is a National Nature Reserve, a Site of Special Scientific Interest and a Special Area of Conservation, with a fragile ecology. It is not a normal municipal park. Fauna and flora of all kinds, both common and rare, live here.

Also remember other users. The bulk of complaints received by park management are made by one type of user about another - about cyclists going too fast, car drivers behaving aggressively, dog walkers not picking up after their dogs, and so on. The Park is an asset to us all, but only if we are considerate and tolerant of each other. The priority in the Park is first wildlife, then pedestrians, domestic animals, cyclists, and cars. Always give way to others in that order.

The eight Royal Parks have a common set of regulations which set out what visitors should and shouldn't do (see the box below). In addition, The Royal Parks publishes a series of leaflets on activities such as cycling and dog walking, and on wildlife such as deer, and trees. These are available at the Visitor Centre or at the Park offices at Holly Lodge.

Under Royal Parks Regulations it is an offence to:

Interfere with plants or fungi
Climb or interfere with a tree
Fish or take birds' eggs
Worry or injure an animal or bird
Feed or touch a deer
Drop or leave litter
Fail to remove dog faeces
Fail to keep a dog under control or (where required) on a lead
Permit a dog to chase, or worry deer
Light a fire (including barbecues)
Cycle or roller skate except on designated paths
Ride, drive or cycle dangerously or at night without lights
Drive above the 20 mph speed limit
Park a car other than in a car park
Play games or sport, fly a kite or model aircraft except in designated areas

It is also an offence to:

Land a helicopter
Graze an animal
Use a metal detector
Play a musical instrument
Camp
Use an amplified apparatus
Discharge a firearm
Wash or dry any piece of clothing
Take part in a display or parade
Carry on a trade
Make a public speech
Bathe in a pond
Tow or leave a caravan
Exhibit a notice or advertisement
Collect or solicit money

(Note: some of these things can be done with permission)

The full regulations can be found on (www.royalparks.org.uk)

Wildlife

Whatever you are doing in the Park, please be considerate of the wildlife. In particular:

● Don't interfere with trees or plants, or take things out of the Park. This includes any wood, fungi and mushrooms (which are important to trees and provide food for wildlife), deer antlers (which are consumed by the deer and other animals), sweet chestnuts (which are valuable food for the deer), and grasses or flowers (some of which are specially protected).

● Don't interfere with wildlife habitats. Please don't move dead or decaying wood or build a house with it; this dries out the wood and kills the beetles and other wildlife that live in it, including some rare species. Don't interfere with birds' nests, stamp on anthills (the young ants grow up in the domes which are warmed by the sun), or chase ducks or swans.

● Don't get too close to deer, particularly with children; the deer may feel they are being threatened (especially if they have young), or something (especially a dog) may spook them making them run towards you. You should stay at least 150 feet (50m) from them. Please don't walk through the herd. If the deer are sitting on the ground they are digesting food, so don't disturb them. If you see a calf or fawn in the undergrowth, don't approach it, it is not lost; its mother has hidden it there while she collects food and will be back shortly (indeed she is probably watching you and may attack you to protect her fawn). Also, don't get too close to the swans or geese, they can be very aggressive.

● Don't feed the birds, swans and other wildfowl, especially with bread. Birds and wildfowl don't naturally eat bread. Each bird species has a particular diet, and many are used to eating seeds, berries and pulses. Please don't feed the deer (yes, some people do); they have difficulty digesting human food, and it encourages them to approach humans.

● Don't leave litter. This includes food from your picnic and other bio-degradable matter, which can affect the ecology of the Park. Take food back home and put non-food litter in a bin. The Royal Parks employs a team of litter pickers, but they cannot pick up everything and deer ingest litter, especially very small pieces that they have difficulty separating from grass. Post-mortem examinations of Park deer (e.g. after one has died from an accident) often reveal quantities of human litter in their stomachs that they have not been able to digest. On occasion deer have died from indigestible litter clogging up their stomach.

● Don't light a barbecue, or bring a portable barbecue with you. It is tempting to do so, particularly when a hollow tree may shield it from the wind. But every year there are ancient oaks badly harmed by barbecues and in the summer there is the risk of grassland fire.

Walking

You can walk anywhere in the Park, except in the enclosed plantations (although some have paths through them). The Park is eight miles (13km) round and two to three miles (4km) across, which gives plenty of space to walk at will. Pedestrians can go into the Park at night, except during the deer cull. But please follow some "good citizen" rules:

● Keep to the established paths. This avoids disturbing the wildlife, harming grassland, and destroying wildflowers and fungi. In summer, walking through the undergrowth risks being bitten by ticks from which you may get Lyme disease. Avoid areas under trees, if you can. Compaction of the soil is getting bad under some trees and hindering their growth.

● Be aware of other users (e.g. runners and cyclists), and give them space to pass safely. Don't walk three or four abreast on the Tamsin Trail so that cyclists cannot get past without going onto the grass (and don't then complain about them being inconsiderate when they shout at you to move!).

Dogs

The open spaces of Richmond Park are wonderful for walking dogs. Dogs have the freedom to run off the lead more and owners can see and control their dogs relatively easily.

However, dogs have a significant impact on nature in the Park. The way they root around disturbs small mammals and invertebrates; for this reason hares which (unlike rabbits) spend all their time above ground, have disappeared from the Park (the last was seen in 1972). There are some important do's and don'ts for dog walkers:

● Always clean up your dog waste. Dog waste is unpleasant and unhygienic for other Park users. Also, dog faeces are relatively rich in nutrients from dog food and damage the Park's acid grassland which thrives on low nutrient soil (deer eat only grass and other flora, such as chestnuts, so their faeces effectively only recycle nutrients within the Park). In addition, the worming agents used on dogs include pesticides and affect the invertebrates in the soil. Put your dog waste in a sealed bag and take it home or put it in one of the 44 dog waste bins located around the Park. Do not leave the bag on the ground, even behind a tree or bush - someone has to clear it up!

● Be in full control of your dog at all times. Sometimes, it may be enough to have it in sight. At other times you may need to keep your dog on a lead, for example, near deer. In May and June keep your dog under close control around bracken and other undergrowth; each year newly born deer (three in 2010) are mauled by dogs that come upon them unexpectedly.

● Do not allow your dog to chase deer, ducks, geese or swans. There have been prosecutions for dogs chasing deer; some cases involved serious injury to the deer, with some having to be put down. Note also that deer can attack dogs if they get too close, particularly in the late spring when mothers are protecting their young. But a male deer will also attack a dog if it is bothering it too much and the dog usually comes off worse!

● Observe the restrictions on dogs. Dogs are not permitted in Pembroke Lodge or its gardens. They have to be kept on a short lead in Isabella Plantation and around Pen Ponds, Adams Pond and Bishops Pond. This restriction was introduced in May 2009, because of an increase in incidents where wildfowl were disturbed or killed - for example, 12 of the 14 cygnets born in the previous year died and dog attacks were thought to be responsible for most of the deaths. Also, in spring and early summer, dogs should be kept on a lead in the Skylark protection zone between Pen Ponds and White Lodge (the Royal Ballet School). This was introduced a few years ago because of the declining number of breeding pairs. Since its introduction, the numbers have increased and Skylarks have now spread to other areas of the Park.

● Do not walk too many dogs. The Park's rule of thumb is that no-one should have more than four dogs, simply because any more makes it difficult to control them if they are off the lead, particularly with deer around, and difficult to pick up after them while keeping control.

Cycling

Cycling is a great way to enjoy the Park, whether you are commuting through the Park, using the road or Tamsin Trail for exercise, or cycling with your family on a nice summer's day. However, cyclists can cause problems for the ecology of the Park and for other road users. There are some clear rules for cyclists:

● Keep to the roads and tracks where cycling is permitted; this is the perimeter road, the road from Sheen Cross to Pen Ponds car park and on to Ham Cross, and the Tamsin Trail and its extension from Ham Gate to Petersham Gate. Cycling is not allowed anywhere else in the Park. Off-road/track cycling erodes the paths (particularly where it creates grooves for water to run down) compacts the ground (hindering growth of flora) and disturbs wildlife. The Park is not a place for mountain biking.

● When cycling on the roads, keep to the 20 mph speed limit everywhere, even downhill. Don't overtake cars when they are doing 20 mph; it is dangerous and irritates drivers (you can hardly complain if they behave badly in return). Give way to pedestrians, particularly at crossings, and to wildlife wherever they cross. Many cyclists don't give way, even when cars do. This is particularly bad at the pedestrian crossings at Pembroke Lodge car park, Roehampton Gate car park and Sheen and Ham Cross.

● When cycling on the Tamsin Trail, keep to the 10 mph speed limit. Be considerate of pedestrians and dogs; slow down when you approach them, ring your bell or call out, and thank them if they move out of the way to let you pass. Keep to the gritted area and don't go onto the grass or cut across a loop in the trail; this erodes the Park and disturbs wildlife. The Tamsin Trail is sinuous to make it interesting; if you want a straight ride, use the perimeter roads.

Car Driving

Driving through the Park can be a delight; many drivers say they unwind from work as they commute through it. However, cars create emissions and, although the direct effect of emissions on plant life reduces even a few metres from the road, a constant diffuse 'fall-out' of nitrogen oxide increases nitrogen in the soil, and harms the acid grassland and the wildlife that lives on it. The Park roads are not part of the national road network, and have somewhat different rules, which you should follow:

● Keep to the 20 mph speed limit. This was the limit until the 1960s when it was raised to 30 mph; it was reduced to 20 mph again in 2004. The lower speed limit gives the Park more of a tranquil feel (which many people noticed when the limit was reduced). It is also safer for pedestrians and cyclists, and has reduced markedly the number of deer killed on the roads - from up to 20 a year before 2004 to five a year now. Don't overtake cars which are doing 20 mph; nobody has been killed on the roads in Richmond Park recently, but in 2008 in Greenwich Park a cyclist was killed by a speeding car coming in the opposite direction.

● Give way to wildlife and pedestrians. If deer are crossing the road, stop until the whole herd has crossed even if it takes them a while. It is a wonderful sight and surely worth a few minutes' pause in your day. Also stop for pedestrians, particularly at the crossings at each gate, Sheen and Ham Cross, and at Pembroke Lodge and Broomfield Hill car parks. The crossings do not have bright markings because that would be out of place in the Park landscape, but you should still stop at them.

● Park in the car parks. It is tempting to park in other places, especially on busy days where parking spots are difficult to find. But you can be fined for parking outside the car parks or in disabled spaces. The parking area at the bottom of Isabella Plantation is for disabled people only; it is patrolled!

Sports and other activities

The nature of the Park limits the activities available, but there are still plenty of things to do.

● Running is allowed everywhere in the Park, but please follow the same rules as pedestrians. Please keep to established paths, avoid compacted areas under trees, don't go near deer, and don't litter. There are organised races and regular running clubs, but they are limited in number and the paths they can use, to reduce the impact on the ecology of the Park.

● Flying model aircraft is permitted on the Flying Field next to Sheen Cross. Flyers gather at the bench with the notice board next to it. Model boats are not allowed on any of the ponds.

● Organised ball games are not allowed, except on the flat area between Sheen Cross and Roehampton Gate, where there are four rugby pitches which are let out to Rosslyn Park Rugby Club at the weekend.

● Fishing is allowed in Pen Ponds, but you need a licence from the Park offices at Holly Lodge. It is an offence to fish without one.

● Kite-flying is allowed (and is a wonderful sight), but is restricted to areas away from trees and birds. The recommended places are the flat open areas near Ham Gate Pond and opposite Broomfield Hill car park. Please do not fly your kite near deer or model aircraft.

● Horse riding. You can ride on the riding tracks at any time and off-track when the ground is suitable; the Park notice boards say when that is. There are riding schools around the Park where you can hire horses and have lessons.

The Friends of Richmond Park

By Ron Crompton, Chairman, Friends of Richmond Park.

The Friends of Richmond Park is a registered charity dedicated to the conservation and protection of Richmond Park and its peace and natural beauty, and to advancing public education about the Park. It has around 1,500 members. The Friends celebrated its 50th anniversary in March 2011.

The Friends has a range of activities, including:

Walks and courses. Up to 25 walks and courses are held each year. Some walks are general, covering one part of the Park; others have a theme or topic (e.g. veteran trees, deer, birds, butterflies, history). The walks are open to all.

Conservation and ecology. We work with Park management on conservation initiatives and fund projects, such as creating new enclosures to encourage bird life, and a survey of stag beetles.

Education. We have a range of educational activities, including publishing a set of family trails in the Park and an annual photography competition for young people.

Campaigning. The Friends was founded as a campaigning organisation and we continue to campaign (much of it behind the scenes) on conservation, traffic and policing issues, as well as The Royal Parks management and governance. We also work through the Friends' Forum, comprising the Friends organisations for each of the eight Royal Parks, and the Richmond Park stakeholder group.

Volunteering. Friends' volunteers staff the Richmond Park Visitor Centre, which provides the public with information on Park wildlife, history, buildings etc. Other volunteers are involved in practical conservation work in the Park, in a History Project cataloguing and writing up historical material on the Park.

Newsletter. We produce a newsletter three times a year, which has articles on wildlife, history, and management of the Park. It also has a children's page and a news page. We send a monthly e-mail to members with news on the Park and Friends events, and a Park Diary and Isabella Diary.

Planning. We monitor planned developments in and around the Park which will have adverse effects on the Park, and lobby against them. We also propose improvements to the environment of the Park.

Traffic. In keeping with the original reasons for its formation, the Friends is particularly concerned about the impact of traffic on the peace and tranquillity of the Park. We monitor the situation closely, and propose actions to reduce the impact and the conflict between cyclists, cars and pedestrians.

Policing. The Friends works with the Parks Police and Park management on policing the Park. Although crime is very low, there is a large job in enforcing Park regulations; we are also part of the Safer Parks Police Panel.

The Friends website (www.frp.org.uk) has information on the Park and the Friends, including campaigns, photographs and the monthly Park Diary/News, a map of the Park, and Park opening times, all of which can be downloaded by the general public.

The Friends is run completely by volunteers, including an Executive Committe of 12 people, elected annually, and many other people who devote considerable time to helping with walks, conservation projects, education activities, writing for the newsletter and so on.

Membership of the Friends currently costs £6 a year (£10 a year for a household), and you can join by downloading a form from the website, or collecting one from the Visitor Centre.

We would be delighted to see you!

Friends History and Objectives

The Friends was founded in 1961 when there was a public outcry over measures to allow traffic to drive through the Park at night and to increase the speed limit from 20 to 30 mph. As a result of the outcry, the Park gates continued to be closed at dusk, although the speed limit was raised. Subsequent measures to include the Park in the national road system were also successfully resisted. In 2004 the speed limit was reduced back to 20 mph.

Today our objectives are:

1 To promote the conservation, protection and improvement of the natural and physical environment of Richmond Park, and its peace and natural beauty for the benefit of the public and future generations, including by seeking to limit the adverse effects on the Park of policies, developments and activities which may damage the attributes of the Park.

2 To advance the education of the public:
(i) in relation to the Park's status as a National Nature Reserve, Site of Special Scientific Interest and Special Area of Conservation and
(ii) generally in relation to the conservation, protection and improvement of the Park.

Richmond Park - True or False?

1. King Henry VIII waited on the Mound for a signal that Anne Boleyn had been executed at the Tower of London in May 1536.
False. Contemporaneous accounts place the King many miles from Richmond on the day of his wife's execution; he apparently chose to spend that fateful day hunting.

2. Lily Langtry, living at Kingstonhill Place, used to signal to Prince Edward, later to be Edward VII, at White Lodge that she was ready to entertain him.
Almost certainly false. Lily Langtry did stay at Kingstonhill Place (just outside the Park behind Broomfield Hill car park); the Prince was familiar with White House Lodge, having lived there in the 1850s, and she was one of his mistresses. But during the years of their affair the Lodge was occupied by the Duke and Duchess of Teck, and the supposed arrangements for assignations between the two seem unlikely.

3. King George III used to shoot turkeys in the Park.
True. For several years in the 18th Century turkeys were raised in the Park for sport. At one point they reached 3,000 in number. King George III would have them flushed out by dogs and he would then shoot them when they sought refuge in a tree.

4. Richmond Gates were designed by Capability Brown.
False. Although there is a long-standing myth that Capability Brown was the architect, it is clear that the present gates – dating from1798 – are the work of Sir John Soane. Sir John also undertook works to Thatched House Lodge and Pembroke Lodge.

5. The Park contains a magical healing tree.
False. The Park did contain a Shrew Ash, which was said to be magical, but it was destroyed in the storm of 1987. The Shrew Ash was so called because a live shrew was placed in a hole in the trunk which was then filled in, creating its magical properties. The tree was used to heal sick children and animals. A 'shrew mother' passed the child nine times around a wooden bar wedged in the cleavage of the tree, reciting a ritual as she did so. The practice dates from medieval times but was still in use in the nineteenth century.

6. The Park was bombed by the Germans in WWII.
True. In 1943 enemy bombs destroyed The Russell School which had stood inside the Park next to Petersham Gate since 1851.

7. The wall round the Park was built without foundations.
True. The wall was certainly poorly constructed, and large sums had to be spent on its repair even in the early years. In 1659 the City Corporation was told that the wall was *'very much broken downe and decayed'*. The oldest sections of wall now surviving probably date from the mid 18th century.

8. The wall round the Park is a listed building.
True. Much of it is listed Grade II. Many buildings in the Park are listed, although only White Lodge is Grade I.

9. Queen Elizabeth, the Queen Mother, lived in the Park.
True. In 1923 (the year of their marriage) and 1924 the Duke and Duchess of York, later to become King George VI and Queen Elizabeth, lived at White Lodge.

10. Many South African soldiers died in the Park.
True. Upwards of 30 South African soldiers are buried in Richmond Cemetery. They died at a military hospital, located between Bishop's Pond and Conduit Wood, which had been constructed in 1916. It was demolished in 1925.

11. There is a disused WWII air raid shelter in Conduit Wood.
False. The structure commonly referred to as an air-raid shelter covers the well (or 'conduit' which gives the Wood its name), which was created in about 1500 for Henry VII. It supplied fresh water to Sheen Palace which, at about the same time, he re-named Richmond Palace.

12. The Park once housed an Olympic Village.
True. The former barracks near Kingston Gate (which were not finally demolished until 1965), were home to athletes during the 1948 Olympics. They were later used for families displaced during the Suez crisis of 1956.

13. The Park has its own police force.
False. The Royal Parks Constabulary, which covered all the Royal Parks, was disbanded in 2004. Policing is now carried out by the Metropolitan Police Service Royal Parks Operational Command Unit.

14. Bertrand Russell was born in Pembroke Lodge.
False. He came to live with his paternal grandparents at Pembroke Lodge in 1876 at the age of four after his parents had died.

15. One of the Park bandstands was blown up by the IRA.
True. In the early 1950s a Victorian-style bandstand was erected near Richmond Gate. It became disused in the 1950s and was moved in 1975 to Regent's Park. On 20 July 1982 the IRA detonated a bomb hidden underneath the bandstand, killing seven men of the Royal Green Jackets.

16. Richmond Park is associated with three British Prime Ministers.
True. Sir Robert Walpole, the first ever Prime Minister (1721 onward), hunted frequently in the Park and took all relevant decisions about it, although his son was nominally in charge as Ranger. Henry Addington (later Lord Sidmouth) became Prime Minister in 1801 and moved into White Lodge the following year, where he lived until his death in 1844; he planted many woods, including Sidmouth Wood, between 1823 and 1830. Lord John Russell became Prime Minister in 1846 and moved into Pembroke Lodge in 1847, where he died in 1878; many Cabinet meetings were held there.

17. Nelson sketched out his battle plans for Trafalgar in red wine during a dinner at White Lodge.
True. Records at the Ballet School show that Nelson visited White Lodge in September 1805 as the guest of Lord Sidmouth, the Prime Minister. The Battle of Trafalgar, at which Nelson was fatally wounded, was to take place the following month. There is a "Nelson Room" to commemorate his visit.

18. There are still traces of medieval features in the Park.

True. There are traces in many places. For example, in the northern part of the Park there is a line of oaks to the west of Holly Lodge that marked a medieval field boundary, a path in Barn Wood next to the fence of Two Storm Wood that was a medieval lane from Mortlake to Ham (called Deane's Lane), and just to the west of that traces of ridge and furrow ploughing.

19. Beverley Brook takes its name from beavers once present here.

True. "Bever" means beaver and "ley" is a colloquial form of the Anglo-Saxon word for stream. Beavers were hunted to extinction in the twelfth century.

20. A Communist President stayed in Richmond Park.

True. On his state visit to Britain in 1953, Marshall Tito of Yugoslavia stayed in White Lodge, at that time privately owned. Its location away from the centre of London was considered ideal for security given the Yugoslav exile community in London that opposed Tito's regime.

21. The annual deer cull weeds out the older creatures; the venison from the cull goes to dignitaries or local restaurants.

False. The annual culls in November and February aim to maintain a balanced herd in terms of age and sex, so the cull is across the herd. Under the Royal Warrant system, the venison used to go to a list of nearly 80 dignitaries, including the Queen and local mayors, but this was stopped in 1997, and it is now sold to a national wholesaler and much of it is exported.

22. The first London Marathon started in Richmond Park.

False. The race itself never has, but the idea for the London Marathon was conceived in 1979 by John Disley and Chris Brasher during a conversation in the Dysart Arms pub (opposite Petersham Gate), the base of the Ranelagh Harriers running club. The first London Marathon in 1981 was then organised from the lodge at Richmond Gate.

23. A rock singer is commemorated in the Park.

True. Ian Dury, the leader of the punk/New Wave band The Blockheads, has a bench in his name in Pembroke Lodge gardens. On the back of the bench are the words to Reasons to be Cheerful (their hit in 1979), and the bench has earpiece sockets from which the song can be heard, powered by solar panels.

24. The Park lost more than 1,000 trees in the Great Storm of 1987.

True. The 1987 storm was followed by another severe storm in 1990, in which many trees were also lost. To replace some of the lost trees, Park management created the Two Storm Wood plantation (near Sheen Gate), hence its name.

25. There were executions in the Park in the 18th century.

False. Gallows Pond is located near Kingston Gate, but was named after the gallows that stood just outside the gate, which were used for executing felons convicted at the Kingston Assizes. Gibbet Wood is located opposite Broomfield Hill car park, but refers to the gibbet that used to stand at the top of Kingston Hill, also just outside the Park (a gibbet was a metal frame for holding the corpse of a felon as it slowly disintegrated, as a warning to others).

Richmond Park Facts

Richmond Park is:

> 2,350 acres (950 ha) in area and eight miles (13 km) in perimeter
> The largest enclosed urban park in Europe
> The largest Royal Park and as big as all the other seven combined
> A Site of Special Scientific Interest (1992), a National Nature Reserve (2000) and a European Special Area of Conservation (2005)
> Eight miles (13 km) from the centre of London
> Essentially still a deer park, as it was when it was enclosed in 1637

The Park has:

> 30 ponds, covering 40 acres (16 ha)
> 550 acres (220 ha) of woodland (about a square mile)
> The largest area of acid grassland in London
> 11 gates (six for vehicles and pedestrians, five pedestrians only)
> Seven and a half miles (12 km) of bridle path
> Seven car parks, covering 100 acres (40 ha)
> Eight miles (13 km) of roads open to cars, with a further four miles (6 km) of access roads or pedestrian/cyclists only
> Seven and a half miles (12 km) of the Tamsin Trail
> A 20 mph speed limit on the roads, 10 mph on the Tamsin Trail
> 20 lodges (including Pembroke, White, Holly and Thatched House)
> Two 18-hole golf courses
> Four rugby pitches
> Two cafes and five refreshment points (some seasonal)
> Nine toilet facilities
> 20 notice boards (some have maps also)
> 102 litter bins and 44 dog waste bins
> Three (redundant) underground reservoirs
> Over 150 full-time equivalent staff managing and maintaining it (8 employee, 140 contractors, 7 police)

It is home to:

> 630 deer (330 Fallow and 300 Red)
> About 130, 000 trees (estimates vary), of which 45% are oak
> 1,380 veteran trees of 14 species
> Over 1,350 species of beetle, of which 140 are nationally scarce or threatened
> Over 730 species of butterfly and moth (42 nationally scarce or threatened)
> 450 species of plants and ferns
> Over 400 species of fungi
> Over 150 species of bees and wasps

139 species of spiders
119 species of birds, 57 of which breed in the Park
9 species of bats (out of 17 in the UK)
Numerous mammals such as fox, rabbits, shrew, mouse and vole
Two Shire horses

It is used by:

2.5 million visitors a year (more than any other of the
224 National Nature Reserves in the UK)
8-10 million motorists a year; over 90% of whom pass straight
through it
60 species of migrating birds

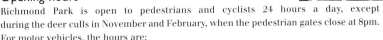

Useful Information

Opening hours

Richmond Park is open to pedestrians and cyclists 24 hours a day, except during the deer culls in November and February, when the pedestrian gates close at 8pm. For motor vehicles, the hours are:

Opening: 7am in summer and 7.30am in winter

Closing: At dusk, which varies according to the time of year - from 4pm in November and December to 9pm in June.

The full opening hours are on The Royal Parks or Friends of Richmond Park websites. If you are still in the Park after closing time, you may face a long drive to the one gate that is left open; if you leave your car overnight it will be ticketed.

Information points

Visitor Centre, located outside and to the right of the gates at Pembroke Lodge. It is staffed entirely by volunteers from the Friends. It offers help and information on all aspects of the Park, with a wide range of maps and leaflets, and various items for sale. All profits from the centre go to conservation projects in the Park.

Open: March to October - Friday to Sunday & Bank Holidays, 10am - 4pm; November to February - Friday to Sunday & Bank Holidays, 10am - 3pm.

Park Office at Holly Lodge, which is also the location of Park management.

Open: All year round - Monday to Friday (closed Bank Holidays), 9am - 4pm.

www.royalparks.org.uk Tel: 020 8948 3209 Email: richmond@royalparks.gsi.gov.uk

Eating & drinking

Pembroke Lodge café provides a comprehensive range of food and drink, with public rooms and a terrace looking out over Petersham and the Thames. It is wheelchair accessible and family friendly. It is also one of the finest venues in west London for weddings and corporate events, seating up to 140 guests. Open: 9am - 5.30pm in the summer; 9.30am - half an hour before dusk in the winter.

www.pembroke-lodge.co.uk Tel: 020 8940 8207.

Email: info@pembroke-lodge.co.uk

Roehampton Café serves a range of snacks, drinks and ice creams, with indoor and outdoor seating. It is located at Roehampton Gate car park.

Open daily: 9am - 5pm summer and 9am until half an hour before dusk in winter. Tel: 020 8876 7933.

Refreshment kiosks are also located at Broomfield Hill and Pen Ponds car parks, and outside Pembroke Lodge gates, serving a range of hot and cold snacks and beverages.

Open: 9am - 6pm in the summer.

Toilet facilities

Toilet facilities are located at Ham Gate, Petersham Gate, next to the Visitor Centre at Pembroke Lodge, Richmond Gate, Sheen Gate, Roehampton Gate café, Robin Hood Gate, Isabella Plantation and Kingston Gate. All except Ham and Petersham Gates have disabled facilities; at Isabella the disabled toilet is at the lower (northern) gate.

Leisure facilities

Riding

Local stables from which rides in Richmond Park take place:

Barnfield Riding School	www.barnfieldriding.org	Tel: 020 8546 3616
Kingston Riding Centre	www.kingstonridingcentre.com	Tel: 020 8546 6361
Stag Lodge Stables	www.ridingin.london.com	Tel: 020 8974 6066
Wimbledon Village Stables	www.wvstables.com	Tel: 020 8946 8579

Cycling

Cycles are available for hire in summer through Parkcycle (located in Roehampton Gate car park), from 10am to 7pm on weekends and during school holidays, and from 10am to 5pm on weekdays and outside holidays. At selected peak times, a secondary hire point is available in the car park adjacent to Pembroke Lodge.
www.parkcycle.co.uk   Tel: 0705 020 9249

Fishing

Fishing is allowed in Pen Ponds, from June 16 to March 14, by paid permit available from Holly Lodge (concessions for children and pensioners).
Tel: 020 8948 3209

Golf

There are two 18-hole courses in Richmond Park, used for both 'pay and play' and for golf clubs and societies. There is also a 16-bay driving range and a large pro-shop. All golfing facilities are accessed via Roehampton Gate car park, although there are plans to redesign the golf courses with access off the A3.
Tel: 020 8876 3205/020 8876 1795

Education

The Holly Lodge Centre

'Special needs in a special place'. The Centre provides a range of 'hands on' activities related to the natural environment and heritage of Richmond Park for people of all ages and abilities, but particularly for those with special needs. Activities are group-based and those for children are designed for Key Stages 1 and 2.
www.thehollylodgecentre.org.uk Tel: 020 8940 8730 or 0845 438 3103
Email: hlcinfo@thehollylodgecentre.org.uk

The Royal Ballet School and Museum

The White Lodge Museum and Ballet Resource Centre, housed in White Lodge, is the first dedicated ballet museum in the UK. The museum covers the daily life of students at The Royal Ballet School, the history and development of Classical ballet and, in parallel, the story of White Lodge itself. Opening times are Tuesdays and Thursdays 1.30-3.30pm during term time, although alternative visiting hours may be arranged for groups of 10-30 people. All visits must be booked in advance.
Phone 020 8392 8440 or see www.royal-ballet-school.org.uk.

The Nature Collection is a 'hands on' collection of feathers, animal bones and photography, which portrays the diversity of British wildlife, particularly in Richmond Park. The collection can be brought into schools, clubs or community halls, or set up as a display stand at exhibitions.
See www.thenaturecollection.co.uk or contact Susanna Ramsey at
susanna@ thenaturecollection.co.uk.

Ecology and Wildlife Groups

Richmond Park has a very active Wildlife Group, led by volunteer experts but including Park staff and members of all levels of knowledge and skills. It has sub-groups which focus on particular areas of ecology, including:

Butterfly Group, which does regular recording of butterflies and moths

Bird Group, which undertakes the annual recording of bird species in the Park

Flora Group, which has been carrying out a survey of the flowering plants and flowers in the Park since 1999

Beetles Group, who are building on earlier surveys of Stag beetles

If you are interested in joining or contributing to the Group, you can contact them by email at richmond@royalparks.gsi.gov.uk with 'Wildlife Group' in the subject line, or by telephone on 020 8948 3209.

Police

There are two numbers for reporting an incident in Richmond Park to the police: If it is an emergency phone 999.   If it is a non-emergency phone 0300 123 1212.

Both numbers take you through to the Metropolitan Police control centre, which will despatch the police to the incident. There is a two-man response team presence in the Park from opening time to 10pm.

Photographs of the Park

The following photographers have kindly contributed their photographs to this book:

Sarah Cuttle: She provided pictures of Pembroke Lodge and Isabella gardens, and is a leading garden photographer. See www.sarahcuttle.co.uk

Kerry Davies: A professional photographer with photographs from many parts of the world, including a set of Richmond Park. See www.wabisabipix.com

Steve Morgan: He has a collection of photographs of Richmond Park and the surrounding area. See his website www.richmondparklondon.co.uk

Susanna Ramsey: Her photographs are part of her educational collection which can be seen at www.thenaturecollection.co.uk

Alex Saberi: He is a wildlife and travel prize-winning photographer, with a portfolio of photographs of Richmond Park, from which the Guide's cover (and other) photos are taken. See http://alexsaberi.com

Andrew Wilson: He has published "Wild in the City", a book of photographs of open spaces in south-west London, including Richmond Park, from which many of the photographs in this Guide have been taken. See www.unity-publishing.co.uk or e-mail aw@unity-publishing.co.uk.

The Royal Parks: Its online store has photographs and maps of Richmond Park and other Royal Parks. www.royalparksstore.org.uk

Friends of Richmond Park

The Friends has a range of activities which are described in a previous chapter of this Guide. Please see www.frp.org.uk for:

Forthcoming walks and courses, and how to book for them

News of the Park and the Friends

How to become involved with the Friends, including volunteering to help with the Visitor Centre or conservation projects, or a downloadable membership application form

Opening hours and a downloadable map of the Park.